Ernest Mandel was educated at the Free University of
Brussels, the Paris Sorbonne and the Free University of Berlin,
where he received his PhD. He lives in Brussels and has long
been active in the Belgian labour movement; he is a leading
member of the Fourth International. Ernest Mandel has
written extensively on political economy. His main works
include *Marxist Economic Theory, Late Capitalism, Introduction
to Volumes I, II and III of Capital, The Second Slump* and *The
Long Waves of Capitalist Development*.

To the memory of Gisela
(20 June 1935 – 14 February 1982)
Who gave me sixteen years of love and companionship
And to whom spontaneity and generosity towards
All human beings came as natural as breathing

Ernest Mandel

Delightful Murder
A social history of the crime story

University of Minnesota Press Minneapolis

Note: Page references in the text refer to
books listed in the bibliography.

Published by the University of Minnesota Press
2037 University Avenue Southeast, Minneapolis MN 55414.

Cover designed by Clive Challis A.Gr.R

Printed in Great Britain

Library of Congress Cataloging-in-Publication Data
Mandel, Ernest.
 Delightful murder.

 Reprint. Originally published: London : Pluto
Press, 1984.
 Bibliography: p.
 Includes index.
 1. Detective and mystery stories — History and
criticism.   2. Literature and society.   I. Title.
[PN3448.D4M34 1986]   809.3′872   85-8679
ISBN 0-8166-1463-6
ISBN 0-8166-1464-4 (pbk.)

Contents

Preface

Let me confess at the outset that I like to read crime stories. I used to think that they were simply escapist entertainment: when you read them, you don't think about anything else; when you finish one, you don't think about it again. But this little book is itself proof that this way of looking at it is at least incomplete. True enough, once you finish any particular crime novel, you stop being fascinated by it; but equally, I, for one, cannot help being fascinated by the enormous success of the crime story as a literary genre.

This is obviously a social phenomenon: millions of people in dozens of countries in all continents read the crime story. Not a few of their authors and quite a number of capitalist publishers have become millionaires by producing that peculiar commodity. They have guessed right about the needs it satisfies as a use-value — or to put it in current parlance, they have correctly gauged its demand curve. Why is this so? What is the origin of these needs? How have they changed over the years, and how are they related to the general structure of bourgeois society? These are some of the questions I will try to answer.

My approach is that of the classical dialectical method as developed by Hegel and Marx. This is how Hegel described it in treating a similar problem:

> When we look at the totality of our existence, we find in our common consciousness the greatest variety of interests and the ways of satisfying them. First of all, there is the broad area of physical needs; the great worlds of crafts [and manufacture], in their broad enterprise and interconnections, as

well as trade, navigation and the technical arts, labour [to satisfy these needs]. Further up [we find] the realm of law and of the laws, the life of the family, the separation of the estates, the whole encompassing field of the state. Further on [we find] the need for religion, which can be found in every heart and which receives satisfaction in church life. And, finally, [there is] the practice of science, itself subdivided into numerous intertwined branches, that is, the totality of knowledge and understanding which encompasses everything.

And when a new need appears the question is posed of the inner necessity of such a need in relation to the other areas of life and of the world. For at first sight, we can do nothing but register the existence of this new need, we cannot immediately explain it. Such an explanation demands further analysis. What science demands [from us] is to understand the *essential inner relation* [of the new need to the rest of life] *and their mutual necessity*. (page 137 ff., author's translation, emphasis added)

Well, am I no more than a victim of bourgeois ideology being sucked into the vortex along with millions of other unfortunates, constructing an elaborate rationalization for a simple idiosyncratic vice? Personal experience, and my failure to feel guilt for indulging in a pleasure proscribed by the Pharisees (for revolution, like religion, has its Tartuffes), have led me to enquire into that most difficult and complex riddle of social theory: how do the laws of individual psychology intersect the great curves of social ideology and of social evolution as a whole?

Because I have dealt with the history of the crime story as *social* rather than literary history, I have deliberately ignored at least one important dimension: the personality, character and lives of most of the authors. There are simply too many of them. To have considered the supply side of the story along with its demand side would have made the task unmanageable. Only in a few cases have I strayed from this course and considered the individual psychology of the crime writer.

But there is another reason for disregarding the personalities, if not the ideas, of the authors. To a large extent, the genre belongs to that portion of literary output that the Germans call *Trivialliteratur*, which involves no small amount of 'mechanical writing', when authors compose, decompose, and recompose story lines and characters as if on a conveyor belt. The personality of the authors in such cases is relevant only in that it makes them able and willing to write in such a way.

To those who consider it frivolous for a Marxist to spend time analysing crime stories, I can only offer this final apology: historical materialism can – and should – be applied to all social phenomena. None is by nature less worthy of study than others. The majesty of this theory – and the proof of its validity – lies precisely in its ability to explain them all.

1. From hero to villain

The modern detective story stems from popular literature about 'good bandits': from Robin Hood and Til Eulenspiegel to Fra Diavolo and Vulpius's Rinaldo Rinaldini to Schiller's *Die Räuber* and *Verbrecher aus verlorener Ehre*. But there has been a dialectical somersault. Yesterday's bandit hero has become today's villain, and yesterday's villainous representative of authority today's hero.

The tradition of bandit stories is a venerable one in the Western world, dating back at least to social movements contesting feudal regimes, and receiving powerful impetus with the onset of the decay of feudalism and the rise of capitalism in the sixteenth century.

In *Primitive Rebels* (1959) and *Bandits* (1969), Eric Hobsbawm has shown that 'social bandits' are robbers of a special type, whom the state (and the oppressor classes) regard as outlaws but who remain within the bounds of the moral order of the peasant community. But this literary tradition is ambiguous, to say the least. Anton Blok has convincingly demonstrated that these rebels were in fact anything but do-gooders and were quite capable of viciously exploiting the peasantry while allying themselves with local landlords against the central power. Of course, it is easier for a peasant to deal with bandits of this sort than with nobles and merchants, which is why the peasants would not support the authorities against these primitive rebels.

Nathan Weinstock, on the other hand, has shown that these bandits were not harbingers of the bourgeois-democratic revolution, nor even agrarian reformers. They were pauperized and lumpenized pre-proletarians, wanderers and waylayers, their qualities and defects quite different from those of the bourgeois or the wage-earner. They embodied a populist, petty bourgeois rebellion against both feudalism and nascent capitalism. This is one of the reasons why the tradition of tales of rebels and bandit dramas is so broad in world literature, not at all limited to Western society. In the Asian mode of production, it led to the Chinese epic masterpiece of the twelfth century, *Shuihu-Zhuan* (On the River's Coast).[1] But it is significant that Spain, the country that gave the bandit story its name as a literary genre – the picaresque novel – was where the decay of feudalism was deepest and where the process of its decline was more protracted, leaving society in an impasse for centuries. (Italian literature reflected a similar, though less pronounced, stagnation.)

On the other side of the Atlantic – where there was no feudal social order but where English absolutism reigned, with all its arbitrariness – populist revolt with 'good bandits' also appears in real life:

> Peter Kerrivan was an Irish boy who in the mid 1700s had been impressed into the English navy, where he was treated as cruelly as a slave. He jumped ship in Newfoundland and became leader of a band of Irish outlaws, themselves either victims of press gangs or indentured servants who had been abducted from Ireland and sold like animals to wealthy English merchants off the Newfoundland coast.
> They became known as the Masterless Men ... The English sent many expeditions of marines against these men, but inevitably their forays ended in bog or bush, along blind trails prepared for them by Kerrivan's men.[2]

Interestingly, Sigmund Freud showed great preference for good bandit stories, and according to Peter Brückner, (*Freuds Privatlektüre*, Köln 1975) drew a parallel between psychoanalysis and the picaresque novel which was like a mirror of society from below, dragged along the streets.

But although the 'good bandit' expressed a populist and not a bourgeois revolt against the feudal order, the revolutionary bourgeoisie could nevertheless share that bandit's sense of injustice in the face of extreme forms of tyrannical and arbitrary rule. In much of Europe and Latin America, the struggle against the spirit of the Inquisition and against torture was the quintessence of the liberal battle for human rights. The lifelong fight of the Italian liberal Alessandro Manzoni against torture, well into the nineteenth century, is justly renowned. Less widely known is the horror of semi-feudal justice into the early nineteenth century even in western Germany, along the Lower Rhine. This decree, for example, issued in 1803, uses language that foreshadows Nazi terminology:

> Whereas we see that the aforementioned gypsy people, in spite of all efforts and precautions, have not yet been exterminated, but have succeeded in spreading from one place to another in small or large bands, and have gone so far as to resist arrest, that therefore it is time to achieve their total extermination.
>
> As soon as one of them is caught for the first time in an evil act or found not to have been stigmatized with the letter 'M' on his back a relapse shall irremediably lead him to the gallows.
>
> A stigmatized gypsy, thereby unmistakably recognized as such, must leave the territory within fourteen days (which are allowed him for departure), at the penalty of the gallows whether the stigmata have been applied in this territory or elsewhere. If the gypsy returns to this territory after departure, he shall be hanged.
>
> These rules shall apply also to gypsy women and youths having reached the age of eighteen years, as they attach themselves heedlessly to the aforementioned bands and follow them, and live by armed robberies and theft.
>
> In general all vagrants, among which have to be counted also vagrant musicians and actors, as well as the beggar-jews and all foreign beggars, must leave the territory within four weeks of the publication of the present decree.

It is not illogical, then, that liberal and revolutionary bourgeois authors should have identified with and excused the revolt of the noble bandit against inhuman law and order sustained by a system they themselves sought to overturn. They could not, of course, condone attacks on private property or the murder of people of property (though the murder of tyrants was another story), but they could well understand that such acts of desperation sprang from an unjust social order and its irrational political institutions. Once these were extirpated, Reason would rule society and crime would wither away. Fire had to be concentrated on the rotten Establishment, and not on those who challenged it, albeit romantically and, ultimately, ineffectively.

The tradition of social protest and rebellion expressed in the bandit stories emerged from a mythified history and lingered on in folk tales, songs and forms of oral lore. But it was welded into literature by authors of middle class, bourgeois, or even aristocratic origin: Cervantes, Fielding, Le Sage, Defoe, Schiller, Byron, Shelley. Their works were written essentially for an upper class public – quite naturally, since they were the only ones apt to buy books at the time.

Alongside the novels of these authors, however, a literary activity of much wider popular appeal arose: the broadsheets read and sold at markets, the famous *Images d'Epinal*; the widely sold *complaintes*; the popular chronicles like the *Newgate Calendar*; the popular melodrama, which attained its greatest heights in the Paris theatres of the Boulevard du Temple. These chronicles differ from the bandit stories, for they generally reflect a pre-capitalist society based upon petty commodity production. Their ideology is still semi-feudal, the unspoken model being an integrated Christian society in which, as Stephen Knight has pointed out, wrongdoers are outcasts who refuse to perform honest labour in an honest community. They can be redeemed, however, if they embrace the fundamental Christian values. Their punishment in the various stories represents an appeal to the community to conform to these values.

A society like this can still deal with its malefactors without specialists – or at least its ideologues think it can. There is no need for a police or detective hero in these yarns, only a good lesson in Christian piety at the end. By the eighteenth century, of course, this was fast becoming anachronistic, and some of the *Newgate Calendar* stories are already showing the first deviations from the rules.

In the nineteenth century, the Boulevard du Temple was called the Boulevard du Crime. Many of the most popular melodramas were concerned with crime. There is little mystery about the reason why. For two centuries, the semi-feudal state had barred the development of a popular theatre. Meanwhile, the eighteenth-century press had done its best to conceal from the broader public the reality of rising crime on the streets of the French capital. At the end of the century, Sébastien Mercier could write, 'The streets of Paris are secure, night and day, with the exception of a few incidents.' But he added, 'They hide or suppress all the scandalous delinquency and murders that might frighten people and demonstrate the lack of vigilance of those responsible for the security of the capital.' Theodore Zeldin, who quotes this passage, concludes that a century later the situation was just the opposite. The Paris press reported 143 night assaults during the month of October 1880 alone. By 1882, the populace had become so anxious that cafes were forbidden to remain open past 12.30 a.m.

But this evaporation of a sense of security had occurred among the petty bourgeoisie and the literate layers of the working class well before it did among the upper classes and high society. While rich neighbourhoods remained relatively safe through the early years of the century, the poor ones were far less protected. The number of persons condemned for crimes in Paris rose from 237 per 100,000 inhabitants in 1835 to 375 in 1847 and 444 in 1868. By the beginning of the nineteenth century, professional criminals, unknown in the eighteenth century, had become a reality.

Balzac estimated that during the Restoration there were about 20,000 professional criminals in Paris (out of a total population of about a million and a quarter), and they faced a military garrison of approximately equal size. He related the rise of professional criminals to the rise of capitalism and the consequent emergence of unemployment. 'Each morning', he wrote in his *Code des Gens Honnêtes*, 'more than twenty thousand people [in Paris] awake with no idea of how they will eat at noon.' It was hardly surprising, he added, that such circumstances led to the emergence of a class of professional criminals. Indeed, as early as 1840, the writer H.A. Fregier was moved by the agglomeration of a miserable mass of paupers around Paris to publish a book entitled *Des Classes*

Dangereuses de la Population dans les Grandes Villes.

Rising street crime could no longer be ignored. The widening of press freedom made it increasingly impossible to conceal, and some sectors of the bourgeoisie did not want to conceal it in any case. The new popular theatre and popular press were, after all, businesses, and why should they not try to increase their profits and accumulate capital by catering to the public's taste for nerve-tingling stories about murders, real or imagined? Thus it was that Paris saw the proliferation not only of the melodramas dealing with crime, but also of the widest possible sensationalist publicity given to real-life murder stories in the yellow press, like that of the widow Chardon and her son, killed in December 1834 by Lacenaire, who would be immortalized after the second world war in the film *Les Enfants du Paradis*. Sometimes there was even a dramatic encounter of fact and fiction, as when Mme Sénépart, the widow of the former director of the Théâtre de l'Ambigu, was murdered by a medical student in 1835 in her flat at number 24 Boulevard du Temple.

The rising preoccupation with crime is best exemplified by Thomas De Quincey's *On Murder considered as one of the Fine Arts*, which appeared in 1827 (the postscript was added in 1854). De Quincey had been editor of the *Westmoreland Gazette* in 1818 and 1819, and had filled its columns with stories about murders and murder trials. In his 1827 essay he actually insisted upon the delectation with murder and speculation about whodunit among 'amateurs and dilettantes', thereby opening the way to Edgar Allan Poe, Gaboriau and Conan Doyle. He also initiated the link between popular journalism and writing about murder, which would involve Dickens, Poe, Conan Doyle and so many other crime story writers, up to Dashiell Hammett, E. Stanley Gardner and other contemporaries.

Similarly, the rising preoccupation with crime among the middle classes and the upper layers of the working class soon began to have an impact on the great novelists of the day, especially Balzac, Victor Hugo, Charles Dickens, Alexandre Dumas and even Dostoevsky. In part, this gave expression to genuine social concerns and deeper ideological motivations. But there were also material reasons why the novelists turned to crime stories: financial difficulties, the search for a wider audience, the possibility of receiving lush payments from the new popular magazines, the rise of the *feuilleton* – serial story – in which writers like Eugène Sue (whose *Mystères de Paris* Karl Marx analyzed at length), Ponson du Terrail, and Paul Feval were winning great popular success. In the melodramas, and more especially in the *feuilletons*, the 'good bandit' living at the fringes of society still prevailed. But the great novelists betrayed no romantic admiration for the 'good bandit'. They treated criminals as social nuisances pure and simple. The bourgeoisie, no longer revolutionary, was now in power. On the other hand, awareness of social injustice, of the antagonism between rich and poor, and of the hypocrisy of dual morality, remained very real. (In Victor Hugo's *Les Misérables* the police act very differently towards a rich bourgeois annoying a poor woman and that same woman defending herself. The young Disraeli's theme of 'Two Nations' is another instance.)

This concern was present quite independently of the political views or commitments of the various authors. Balzac was an arch-conservative, but acutely aware of the social causes of the spread of crime. They thought that once having been punished, criminals ought to be able to redeem themselves, something society seemed loathe to permit. The central hero of *Les Misérables* is the ex-convict Jean Valjean, and the hero of *La Comédie Humaine* is Jacques Collin, alias Trompe-la-Mort, alias l'Abbé Carlos Herrera, alias Vautrin.

To be sure, these are no longer 'good bandits' in the old sense. Their criminal acts are treated as the deeds of scoundrels. But they have hearts of gold nonetheless, and redeem themselves through parental devotion to more or less innocent young victims of upper-class cruelty or police persecution. They are figures of transition: no longer the noble bandits of yesteryear, but not yet the heartless villains of the twentieth-century detective story.

Even more significant as a transitional figure is Rodolphe, in Eugène Sue's *Mystères de Paris*. He is both an individual avenger of injustice, and thus a forerunner of the future master detective, and a fugitive, if not from justice, then at least from a sector of the authorities, and thus an heir of the noble bandit who takes from the wicked rich and gives to the deserving poor. Ponson du Terrail's immensely popular hero Rocambole offers a similar combination of qualities. At first a delinquent, indeed the very embodiment of evil, and killed off by his author in *Les Exploits de Rocambole* (1859), he magically reappears in *La Résurrection de Rocambole* (1863) as a fearless detective and Knight of Good.

To understand why this evolution continued, why this literary genre did not stop at that transitional phase but instead went all the way in the transformation of the noble bandit into the evil criminal, we must examine both the objective function of popular literature and its ideological metamorphosis during the last half of the nineteenth century.

The German literary historian Klaus Inderthal called popular literature a 'prosaic reflection' of bourgeois society, 'unreflected (or reflectionless) literature'. It responds to a need for distraction – for entertainment – sharpened by the increased tension of industrial labour, generalized competition, and city life (hence the proximity of popular literature and popular theatre, and the even closer relation with the birth of cinema and television). It answers a need to overcome the growing monotony and standardization of labour and consumption in bourgeois society through a harmless (since vicarious) reintroduction of adventure and drama into daily life. The romantic, bucolic setting of the old bandit stories becomes increasingly meaningless in this context. What Jules Janin said about the Paris melodrama applies equally well to the mystery novel: 'It [the government] tolerates these little plays for the people's amusement.'

It is also fuelled by an anxiety that is more deep-seated, a contradiction between biological impulses and social constraints that bourgeois society has not solved, and indeed cannot solve. In the eighteenth century it took the form of a contradiction between nature and an unreasonable social order. Now it has become a contradiction between nature and bourgeois – reasonable – society. Most important of all, then, the rising place of crime stories in popular literature corresponds to an objective need for the bourgeois class to reconcile awareness of the 'biological fate' of humanity, of the violence of passions, of the inevitability of crime, with the defence of and apology for the existing social order. Revolt against private property becomes individualized. With motivation no longer social, the rebel becomes a thief and murderer. The criminalization of attacks on private property makes it possible to turn these attacks themselves into ideological supports of private property.

Is it contradictory to maintain that the need for distraction from monotony lies at the root of the popularity of the crime story, and that simultaneously a deep anxiety lies buried within that need? I think not. In a brilliant flash of intuition, Walter Benjamin once observed that a traveller reading a detective story on a train is temporarily suppressing one anxiety with another. Travellers fear the uncertainties of travel, of reaching their destinations, of what will happen when they get there. They temporarily suppress (and thus forget) that fear by getting involved in innocent fears about crime and criminals that, they well know, are unrelated to their personal fate. ('Kriminalromane auf Reisen', *Gesammelte Schriften*, Werkausgabe, vol. 10, pp.381-82)

More fundamentally, Erich Fromm has indicated that the sensation of tedium and monotony, of boredom, is but a manifestation of a deeper anxiety. There are two ways to defeat boredom: to become productive and thereby happy, or to escape its manifestations. The latter is the characteristic method of the average contemporary person, who ceaselessly pursues amusements and distractions of the most varied forms. Feelings of depression and boredom are most striking when one is alone with oneself or those closest to one. All our amusements are designed to escape that boredom through one of the many flights open to us. More to the point, Fromm writes:

> Millions are fascinated daily by reports about crime and by crime stories. They flock to films whose two main themes are crime and misfortune. This interest and this fascination are not merely the expression of bad taste and a craving for scandal, but correspond to a deep yearning for the dramatization of the ultimate thing in human life, namely life and death, by crime and punishment, struggle between man and nature. (pp.142-43, 194, translated from the German)

The dramatization of crime that so innocently tingles the nerves of alienated people can be bent to the purpose of defending private property because this defence takes shape in an unreflected way.[2] People don't read crime novels to improve their intellect or to contemplate the nature of society or the human condition, but simply for relaxation. It is thus perfectly possible for socially critical and even socially revolutionary readers to enjoy detective stories without altering their views.[3] But the *mass* of readers will not be led to seek to change the social status quo by reading crime stories, even though these stories portray conflicts between individuals and society. The criminalization of these conflicts makes them compatible with the defence of bourgeois 'law and order'.

There, in a nutshell, is the objective meaning of the rise of the detective story in the middle of the nineteenth century, at a particular point in the development of capitalism, pauperism, criminality, and primitive social revolt against bourgeois society. And at a particular stage of the evolution of literature too. The popular detective story, catering to wide sections of the middle classes and to literate upper layers of the working class, was able to achieve what the bourgeois novel, with its restricted audience, never could accomplish. With the rising need of the bourgeoisie to defend instead of attack the social order, the noble bandit is transformed into the evil criminal. No less a person than Karl Marx observed:

> A philosopher produces ideas, a poet poems, a clergyman sermons, a professor compendia, and so on. A criminal produces crimes. If we look a little closer at the connection between this latter branch of production and society as a whole, we shall rid ourselves of many prejudices. The criminal produces not only crimes but also criminal law, and with this also the professor who gives lectures on criminal law and in addition to this the inevitable compendium in which this same professor throws his lectures onto the general market as 'commodities'. This brings with it augmentation of national wealth, quite apart from the personal enjoyment which – as a competent witness, Herr Professor Roscher, [tells] us – the manuscript of the compendium brings to its originator himself.

The criminal moreover produces the whole of the police and criminal justice, constables, judges, hangmen, juries, etc.; and all these different lines of business, which form equally many categories of the social division of labour, develop different capacities of the human spirit, create new needs and new ways of satisfying them. Torture alone has given rise to the most ingenious mechanical inventions, and employed many honourable craftsmen in the production of its instruments.

The criminal produces an impression, partly moral and partly tragic, as the case may be, and in this way renders a 'service' by arousing the moral and aesthetic feelings of the public. He produces not only compendia on Criminal Law, not only penal codes and along with them legislators in this field, but also art, belles-lettres, novels, and even tragedies, as not only Müllner's *Schuld* and Schiller's *Diё Räuber* show, but also *Oedipus* and *Richard the Third*. The criminal breaks the monotony and everyday security of bourgeois life. In this way he keeps it from stagnation, and gives rise to that uneasy tension and agility without which even the spur of competition would get blunted. Thus he gives a stimulus to the productive forces. While crime takes a part of the superfluous population of the labour market and thus reduces competition among the labourers – up to a certain point preventing wages from falling below the minimum – the struggle against crime absorbs another part of this population. Thus the criminal comes in as one of those natural 'counterweights' which bring about a correct balance and open up a whole perspective of 'useful' occupations. (*Theories of Surplus Value*, Part I, pp.387-88)

2. From villain to hero

The archetypal police figure of modern literature is modelled after history's first well-known policeman: Fouché's sidekick Vidocq. Himself a former convicted bandit who pressed many criminals into the service of Napoleon's Ministry of the Interior as informers, Vidocq forged his own legend, not only by his practical villainy, which was virtually unbounded, but also by his mendacious *Mémoires*, published in 1828. Balzac's Bibi-Lupin and Victor Hugo's Inspector Javert were clearly patterned after this elusive and terrifying figure whose actions and mentality alike bore the seeds that would one day germinate in such varied but equally unsavoury characters as J. Edgar Hoover, Heinrich Himmler, and Beria.

In the first part of the nineteenth century, the great majority of the middle classes and the intelligentsia were essentially hostile to the police. In most Western countries, the state apparatus was still, anachronistically, semi-feudal, an institution against which the bourgeois class had to fight (however inconsistently) in its efforts to consolidate its economic and social power. Where the state was already bourgeois – Britain, France, Belgium, Holland, and the infant United States – the liberal bourgeoisie preferred it to remain weak, confident that the laws of the market would suffice to perpetuate its rule. State spending was considered a waste, an unproductive deduction from surplus-value that would do no more than reduce the amount of capital that could be accumulated. The police force was considered a necessary evil, intent on encroaching upon individual rights and freedoms. The weaker it was, the better.

In any case, there was a far more practical reason for hostility to the police. The Bankruptcy Law, at least in Britain, still defined insolvency as a criminal offence. The prison population included many more debtors than murderers, or even thieves. Judges, police and prison officials dealt with debts, bank drafts and bills much more than with crimes of violence. Their main victims were, accordingly, middle class tradespeople and their genteel clientele, as Dickens portrayed so unforgettably in the immortal figure of Mr Micawber and in his novel *Bleak House*.[1] Industrial discipline had not yet sufficiently impressed upon the citizenry that you had no right to spend 21 shillings when your income was only 20. Consumer credit had not yet appeared to take up the slack. So it was not surprising that the middle classes tended to be hostile to the entire system of law and law enforcement.

All that began to change between 1830 and 1848. These were the years of initial working-class revolt against poverty and capitalist exploitation: the uprising of the La Croix-Rousse silk weavers in Lyons in France and of the Silesian cotton weavers in Prussia; the rise of the Chartist movement in Britain; the eruption of insurrection in Paris in June 1848. The violence and sweep of these rebellions struck fear into the bourgeoisie for the first time: perhaps their power would not reproduce itself eternally through the operation of market laws alone. A stronger state and a correspondingly more powerful police force were needed to keep a watchful eye on the lower orders, on the classes that were ever restive, periodically rebellious, and therefore criminal in bourgeois eyes.

In his path-breaking work *Classes Laborieuses et Classes Dangereuses*, the French historian Louis Chevalier writes:

> From the last years of the Restoration to these first years of
> the Second Empire, during which a monumental Paris arose
> out of the ruins of the old city, crime was one of the major
> themes of everything that was written in Paris and about
> Paris. This Paris was criminal above all because of the
> prominent place crime occupied in the daily concerns of the
> people. The fear aroused by crime was constant; neverthe-
> less, it reached its greatest pitch during some cold and
> miserable winters. Even more important than fear of crime,

> however, was public interest in it and in everything about it.
> Beyond these instances of terror and fright, indeed, interest
> in crime was one of the forms of popular culture in these
> times: and also of the people's own ideas, images, and words,
> beliefs, awareness, and manner of speech and behaviour.
> (pp.36-37)

Another change occurred around the same period: crime became an increasingly capitalist enterprise. In 1850 the largest number of criminal indictments issued in France were still for theft, but by 1860 fraud had become the most common offence. Between 1830 and 1880, the number of recorded thefts rose 238 per cent, of frauds 323 per cent, and of confidence tricks 630 per cent (Zeldin, p.165). Petty tradespeople, craftworkers, schoolteachers, low-ranking government functionaries, and peasants doubtlessly hoped to stay out of prison, but they were equally inclined to see those who tried to cheat them out of their meagre savings or small current income put behind bars.

As the prisons were slowly emptied of debtors and filled with an inmate population of crooks, thieves, burglars, thugs and murderers, the social status of agents of law enforcement correspondingly rose. Nevertheless, in the Anglo-Saxon countries in particular, the bourgeoisie had enough self-confidence not to glorify the police. No longer were they evil. They had ceased to be merely necessary and were now regarded as good. The police could keep order, and they would deal effectively with routine crime. Contrary to a widespread misconception, the police in the first detective stories – from Edgar Allan Poe to Arthur Conan Doyle to Mary Roberts Rinehart – were neither Keystone Kops nor burlesque imbeciles. Pedestrian plodders they may have been, but they generally won out in the end. Only in exceptionally complicated cases were the police outwitted.

These police were not rich entrepreneurs or gentlefolk; they were not themselves members of the ruling class, but generally belonged to the lower middle class, if not to that sought after, but scarcely attainable bourgeois dream, the permanently integrated, upper layer of the working class. The self-assertive bourgeoisie had no reason to vaunt the superior intellectual qualities of lower middle class or higher proletarian elements, especially in Britain, where all were supposed to know their place, and in the southern states of the USA (before and after Reconstruction), where 'uppity' members of the lower depths were considered suspect if not downright subversive. The real hero of the criminal detective story therefore had to be not the plodding cop, but a brilliant sleuth of upper-class origins. And that is what Dupin and Sherlock Holmes, Dr Thorndike and Arsène Lupin really are. And also E. Gaboriau's Inspector Lecoq, inspired and guided by Baron Moser: quite an exception for a normal cop.

The very idea of 'outwitting' a criminal, if it is to hold any fascination, implies the existence of both a criminal with superior wits and a detective of even finer craftiness than the outstanding malefactor. The former implication was and remains far from reality. The overwhelming majority of crimes, especially violent ones, actually committed during the nineteenth century in Britain, France, Germany and the United States (not to mention Italy, Spain, Belgium, Holland, Sweden, and Switzerland) bear witness to no stunningly contrived efforts at concealment or frame-up of innocent scapegoats. And if there were any paragons endowed with that peculiar combination of knowledge, sophistication, intelligence and imagination typical of the early super-sleuths, they must have been occupied by endeavours more challenging and satisfying than chasing down criminals.

The original detective stories, then, were highly formalized and far removed from realism and literary naturalism. But more than that, they were not really concerned with crime as such. The crime was a framework for a problem to be solved, a puzzle to be put together. In many cases, the murder occurs even before the story starts. The occasional additional murders committed as the plot unfolds are almost casual, meant either to spur on the investigation of the initial murder or to provide supplementary clues to the murderer's identity. Rarely are they independent acts of homicidal violence intended to stimulate indignation, the passion for punishment, or a sense of revenge.

The real subject of the early detective stories is thus not crime or murder but enigma. The problem is analytical, not social or juridical. As Professor Dove has pointed out, the classical pattern of the detective story is a seven-step sequence first created by Poe and Conan Doyle: the Problem, the Initial Solution, the Complication, the Period of Confusion, the Dawning Light, the Solution, and the Explanation (p.11). In his 'Twenty Rules of the Detective Story' (*The American Magazine*, September 1928), S.S. Van Dine also stresses what he calls 'fair play' towards the reader, which must be shown by the author of a good crime story. The 'battle of wits', in other words, unfolds simultaneously at two levels: between the great detective and the criminal, and between the author and the reader.

In both battles, the mystery is the identity of the culprit, to which the detective and reader alike are to be led by a systematic examination of the clues. But while the story's hero always succeeds, the reader ought not to succeed in outwitting the author. Otherwise the psychological need to which the detective story is supposed to respond is not assuaged: there is no tension, suspense, surprising solution or catharsis.

The art of the detective story is to achieve this goal without cheap tricks. The clues must all be up front. No secret substitution of one identical twin for another is allowed, no secret passages out of rooms supposedly locked from inside. The reader must be surprised when the murderer's identity is revealed, and with no violation of 'fair play'. To surprise without cheating is to manifest genuine mastery of the genre. Agatha Christie is thus aptly called the 'queen of deception'. And indeed, to practise the art of deception while 'playing fair' is the very quintessence of the ideology of the British upper class.

The nature of the original detective story is thus related equally to the functions of popular literature and to the deeper forces operating beneath the surface of bourgeois society. The reduction of crime, if not of human problems themselves, to 'mysteries' that can be solved is symbolic of a behavioural and ideological trend typical of capitalism.

On the market, commodity owners relate to one another through exchange alone. Their relations thus become alienated and reified; they become mere relations between things, which is reflected even in language. A waitress once said to me in a New York restaurant, 'You're the corned beef and cabbage, aren't you?' All human relations in bourgeois society thus tend to become quantifiable, measurable and empirically predictable. They are broken down into components and studied as under a microscope (or through a computer) as though they were physical substances like a piece of metal or a chemical, or objective phenomena like the price fluctuations of some company's stock on the market. The analytical mind holds sway over the synthetic one. No dialectical balance between analysis and synthesis is ever even considered. And what is the mystery story if not the apotheosis of the analytical mind in its purest form?

The greatest triumphs of analytical intelligence were achieved in the natural sciences, in particular in their applications to technology and the construction of mechanical artefacts. The interaction between analytical intelligence, scientific progress, the development of modern industry and transportation on the one hand, and the rise of the capitalist mode of production and distribution on the other has been described so often that it has become a platitude. We find a parallel interaction in the origin and early development of the detective story.

Modern police work was based on primitive but powerful technical innovations like the generalization of records of the addresses and names of citizens (often in the face of great resistance by the targets of that initial reduction of individuals to numbers) and on a mounting use of reports by informers about alleged criminals. In *Splendeurs et Misères des Courtisanes*, Balzac states:

> The police have files, almost always accurate, on all families
> and individuals whose lives are suspect and whose actions are
> blameworthy. No deviation escapes them. The ubiquitous
> notebook, balance-sheet of consciences, is as meticulously
> kept as the accounts of the Bank of France. Just as the Bank
> takes note of the slightest arrears, weighs all credits, assesses
> the capitalists, eyes their operations closely, so the police
> stand guard over the honesty of the citizenry. In this, as in
> court, the innocent have nothing to fear, for action is taken
> only against defaulters. However highly placed a family may
> be, it cannot elude this social providence. The discretion of
> this power, moreover, is as great as its extent. This immense
> quantity of records in the police stations – of reports, notes,

files – this ocean of information, slumbers without motion, deep and calm as the sea. These files, in which the antecedents are analyzed, are no more than bits of information that die within the walls of the Ministry; Justice can make no legal use of them, but finds its way by their light, and employs them thus – no more. (p.377)

But the same Balzac has his hero Jacques Collin exclaim sharply to a prosecutor, 'You take vengeance every day, or believe to avenge society, sir, and yet you ask me to avoid vengeance!' (p.586)

A real breakthrough occurred around 1840 with the invention and rapid spread of photography. Records of both criminals and clues could then be made, kept, and stored for future use. It was not long before the taking and recording of fingerprints followed. It is therefore no accident, as Walter Benjamin noted, that there is a chronological correspondence between the discovery of photography and the origin of the detective story. C.L. Ragghianti has shown that the discovery of photography ruined realism and naturalism in painting for a long period. Pierre Francastel has recalled how the French painter Gustave Courbet, precursor of the Impressionists, began to destroy the 'subject of painting' by representing optical appearances instead of identified objects. It could be added that the development of railways and the changes thus brought about in the perception of landscapes and the movement of images also had their effects. And the detective story is to 'great' literature what photography is to 'great' painting. The detective story is closely related to machinery as well as to perfected analytical intelligence, for the classical detective story is a formalized puzzle, a mechanism that can be composed and decomposed, unwound and wound up again like the works of a clock, itself the classical prototype of the modern machine.

Technically speaking, this new literary genre integrated three elements: the 'reverse story' (*récit à rebours*) developed by Godwin (*Caleb Williams*, 1794); the divination-deduction technique, originated in Persia and introduced into modern literature by Voltaire (*Zadig*), and the *coup de théâtre*, borrowed from melodrama.[2]

In *Caleb Williams* Godwin, political ideologue and precursor of anarchism, created a transitional sort of novel of which Stephen Knight has remarked that it corresponds neither to a Christian organic ideology (semi-feudal, petty commodity production) nor to the individualistic bourgeois ideology of the detective novel. It exhibits a *radical* petty-bourgeois (semi-Jacobin) ideology: the author longs for a small community composed of honest, amicable, and basically equal individuals, in other words, small property owners.

The first great detective story writers were Edgar Allan Poe, Emile Gaboriau, William Wilkie Collins, Arthur Conan Doyle, R. Austin Freeman, Mary Roberts Rinehart, Gaston Leroux, and Maurice Leblanc. But a large number of their contemporaries in England and France could be added to the list.

Poe's *Murders in the Rue Morgue* is considered the first detective story properly so called. This is no doubt true, in the sense that Auguste Dupin, the prototype of the amateur detective, solves the mystery through pure analytical expertise. The idea of an orang-utan as murderer, however, could well be considered somewhat outlandish. Personally, I prefer two other small masterpieces of Poe's, *Thou Art the Man* (1844), which is the first detective story with a 'real' murderer in the classical sense of the word, and *The Purloined Letter* (1845), which deals not with murder but with theft.

In Inspector Lecoq, Emile Gaboriau created a detective who combines Dupin's deductive powers with the painstaking investigation of clues (*Le Crime d'Orcival*, 1867). The French can well argue that the detective story is of French rather than English origin, since Gaboriau, once the secretary of the *feuilletoniste* Paul Feval, is the first to have created a real series of detective novels. It should also be noted that social and political problems are far more prominent in his novels than in the stories of Poe or Conan Doyle, in particular the conflict between monarchist conservative landowners and the liberal bourgeoisie.

One of the most famous detective stories of all time – *The Moonstone*, by William Wilkie Collins – appeared in 1868 in *All the Year Round*, a magazine edited by Charles Dickens. Collins, to quote Benvenuti and Rizzoni, 'conceived the idea of choosing the culprit from among the least suspect characters, and in his works portrayed medical, legal, and police procedural details with complete accuracy.'

Let it be noted in passing that the expression 'detective story' was first used in 1878 by the American novelist Anna Katharina Greene in her book *The Leavenworth Case*. But the real progenitor of the detective story, or at least the person most responsible for its enormous popularity, was of course Arthur Conan Doyle, the creator of Sherlock Holmes (*A Study in Scarlet*, 1887; *The Adventures of Sherlock Holmes*, 1892; *The Memoirs of Sherlock Holmes*, 1894). Indeed, Conan Doyle himself gave a classic description of the attempt to turn criminology into an exact science in *A Study in Scarlet*:

> Like all other arts, the Science of Deduction and Analysis is one which can only be acquired by long and patient study. Before turning to those moral and mental aspects of the matter which present the greatest difficulties, let the inquirer begin by mastering more elementary problems. Let him, on meeting a fellow mortal, learn at a glance to distinguish the history of the man, and the trade or profession to which he belongs. Puerile as such an exercise may seem, it sharpens the faculties of observation, and teaches one where to look and what to look for. By a man's fingernails, by his coat sleeve, by his boot, by his trouser knees, by the callosities of his forefinger and thumb, by his expression, by his shirt-cuffs – by each of these things a man's calling is plainly revealed.

If we add that Conan Doyle had studied medicine at the University of Edinburgh under Professor John Bell – champion of the theory of deductive methodology in the diagnosis of diseases, a man who never tired of telling his students to use their eyes, ears, hands, brain, intuition, and above all their deductive faculties – then the nexus of the original detective story with triumphant bourgeois society, machinery, natural science, and reified bourgeois human relations stands out unmistakably. It is all summed up by the Goncourts in their *Journal* (16 July 1856): 'he [Edgar Allan Poe] ushers in the scientific and analytical literature in which things play a more important part than people.'

Boileau and Narcejac would express the same idea a century later, arguing that the detective story deals primarily with 'men as objects' dominated by fate (p.125). In *The Red Thumb Mark* (1907), R. Austin Freeman, described by Boileau and Narcejac as the creator of the scientific detective story, further develops the attempt to make criminology an exact science. And what the Goncourts said about Poe applies equally to him: he deals more with facts than with people.

The same cannot be said of Mary Roberts Rinehart (*The Circular Staircase, The Great Mistake*), who solved her mysteries through studying atmosphere and psychology more than the painstaking gathering of clues. Nevertheless, her solutions remained essentially games of deductive intelligence. Gaston Leroux's hero Rouletabille, even more than Sherlock Holmes, relies exclusively on his analytical intelligence, distrusting evidence, which he believes can always be misleading (*Le Mystère de la Chambre Jaune*, 1912). Rouletabille is inspired at least in part by Arsène Lupin, created by Maurice Leblanc (*L'Arrestation d'Arsène Lupin*, 1905; *Arsène Lupin, Gentleman Cambrioleur*, 1907) and still the most popular hero of mystery stories apart from Sherlock Holmes. The son of an aristocratic mother, Arsène Lupin is a strange reincarnation of the old 'noble bandit', but with the added qualities of the Great Detective. His exploits combine the detective story's exaltation of analytical prowess and rationality with the vivid action and metamorphoses of identity of the *feuilleton*. He steals from the rich and gives to the poor, in the process defending widows, orphans, and the exploited. A master of disguise and escape, Lupin steals not for money, but, as Benvenuti and Rizzoni note, 'for psychological satisfaction, the pleasure of defying society, of ridiculing its oldest institutions, and of calling attention to its repressive customs'. His favourite victims are usurers, banks, insurance companies, churches, the Treasury, the super-rich, and even Kaiser Wilhelm II, as well as thieves, murderers, blackmailers and spies.

3. From the streets to the drawing room

The inter-war period was the golden age of the detective story. Granted, some of the best works were written in the forties, and a few precursors of Agatha Christie were publishing before 1914. But the first world war may be seen as a watershed between the sort of stories written by Conan Doyle and Gaston Leroux and the great classics of the twenties and thirties.

It is not easy to list the most representative authors of the golden age. Some we will leave aside for the moment because they are more usefully discussed as later developments of the detective story: these are the creators of police-inspector heroes and of spy stories. Others – like Sax Rohmer, E. Philip Oppenheim and Nick Carter – belong in the category of *colportage* literature. Yet others are omitted for subjective reasons: those who I think lacked the skills of plot-construction and suspense-creation and therefore are not sufficiently representative. In sum, I freely admit that the selection is readily open to challenge.

Two books represent the pre-world-war-one transition between the pioneers and the golden age: E.C. Bentley's *Trent's Last Case* (1913) and A.E.W. Mason's *At the Villa Rose* (1910), the first superior to the second (at least in my opinion, not shared by such connoisseurs as Julian Symons). Both novels have all the ingredients of the classics of the golden age, except the rhythm and style of sustained tension. Has the machine-gun staccato of world war one something to do with that transformation?

We would list the classical representatives of the golden age of the detective story this way: Agatha Christie, G.K. Chesterton, Anthony Berkeley (Francis Iles), Dorothy Sayers, Earl D. Biggers, J. Dickson Carr, S.S. Van Dine, Ellery Queen, Margery

Allingham, Rex Stout, Erle Stanley Gardner, Mignon B. Eberhard, Nicholas Blake, Raymond Postgate, and Frances and Richard Lockridge. Edgar Wallace is a borderline case between *colportage* literature and a really creative spirit (he is, after all, the creator of King Kong). Stanislaw-André Steeman, Ngaio Marsh, and Josephine Tey bridge these classics and the police-inspector school, but the nature of their plots places them in the golden age.

It is not easy to summarize the contributions of these authors to the detective story. Reluctantly, we would make the following comments:

Agatha Christie, whose best books include *The Murder of Roger Ackroyd* (1926), *Murder on the Orient Express* (1934), and *The ABC Murders* (1936), as well as *Murder at the Vicarage* (1930), the first Miss Marple story, was a master of the creation and maintenance of suspense.

G.K. Chesterton (*The Incredulity of Father Brown*, 1936; *The Scandal of Father Brown*, 1935), essentially an author of short stories in the mystery field, has the distinction of having introduced metaphysics into the crime novel. His detective, Father Brown, is a priest who bases himself on the 'understanding of sin' and Catholic theology in general to prove that things are not what they seem.

Anthony Berkeley (Francis Iles) is a master of logical deduction, especially exemplified in *The Poisoned Chocolates Case* (1929).

Dorothy Sayers, with her hero Lord Peter Wimsey, introduced both wholesale snobbery and pleasant humour into the detective story (*Unnatural Death*, 1927; *Murder Must Advertise*, 1933).

Earl D. Biggers invented Charlie Chan, a Chinese detective operating in Honolulu (*The Chinese Parrot*, 1926; *Charlie Chan Carries On*, 1930).

S.S. Van Dine (pseudonym of Willard Huntington Wright) was the most erudite of mystery writers, but his erudition made his hero, Philo Vance, an insufferable character (*The Canary Murder Case*, 1927).

J. Dickson Carr tried to rationalize the apparently supernatural, especially in his Gideon Fell stories (*The Emperor's Snuff Box*, 1942). One of his best Sir Henry Merrivale stories is *The Plague Court Murders* (1934).

Ellery Queen (the pen name of two cousins, Manfred D. Lee and Frederick Dannay) was probably the most capable of the lot. But unbridled imagination and lack of self-criticism made their works increasingly bizarre, the situations straining credulity (*The French Powder Mystery*, 1930; *The Devil to Pay*, 1938; *Calamity Town*, 1942; *The Origin of Evil*, 1951).

Margery Allingham was the creator of Albert Campion, prototype of the private detective who conceals his intelligence behind a mask of vacuous imbecility (*Death of a Ghost*, 1934; *Flowers for the Judge*, 1936).

Rex Stout, a master story-teller, was inclined towards purely deductive reasoning, as embodied in his hero, Nero Wolfe (*Too Many Cooks*, 1938; *Might as Well Be Dead*, 1956; *The Doorbell Rang*, 1965).

Erle Stanley Gardner, himself a criminal lawyer, shifted the scene of the detective story to the courtroom in his Perry Mason stories (*The Case of the Shoplifter's Shoe*, 1938). *Top of the Heap* (1952) is one of the best Donald Lam stories, written by Gardner under the pen-name A.A. Fair. Lam's partner, Bertha Cool, is one of the first detectives who is in business for the explicit purpose of making as much money as possible, which she then invests in diamonds.

Mignon B. Eberhard was an American emulator of Agatha Christie, while Ngaio Marsh (*Overtures to Death*, 1948) and Josephine Tey (*The Franchise Affair*, 1948) were British. Tey tried to apply the techniques of the detective story to a real historical mystery: was King Richard III really guilty of the Tower murders (*The Daughter of Time*, 1951)?

Frances and Richard Lockridge introduced the married couple into crime detecting (*The Norths Meet Murder*, 1940). Stanislaw-André Steeman was a gifted Belgian of Polish origin who created Commissioner Wenceslav Vorobeitchek, a police inspector of similar stock. His *L'Assassin Habite au 21* (1940) effectively utilizes a technique already applied by Christie in *Murder on the Orient Express*: a group of murderers each of whom provides the others with an alibi. Raymond Postgate is famous for his novel *Verdict of Twelve* (1940). Nicholas Blake is the creator of the detective Nigel Strangeways.

What characterizes the classics of the detective story and separates them from their precursors as much as from subsequent writers is the extremely conventionalized and formalized character of their plots. To a large extent this marks a return to Aristotle's famous rules for the drama: unity of time, place and action. In all these novels, certain common rules are observed. The number of characters is small, and all of them are present at the scene of the crime – or better still, remain there throughout the novel. In the purest representatives of the classics, the time span is short. The real temporal framework is the time during which the suspected persons stay together, and during which the crime is committed, even though events of the past may well provide the key to the murderer's motivation. The initial murder is the heart of the action, and it occurs at the outset of the story, sometimes even before it begins.

The criminal is a single individual, although there may be accessories, but no conspiracies of the Sax Rohmer, Edgar Wallace, or even Fantomas type, and no arch-villains like Sherlock Holmes's famous adversary Professor Moriarty or Fu Manchu. The culprit is always individual, and is to be guessed by the reader (often on the assumption that the guilty party is the one on whom the least suspicion falls) and unmasked by the detective.

More often than not, the personality of this individual is formalized and conventionalized, generally embodying a single drive or passion that accounts for the crime. The number of these passions is quite limited: greed, revenge, jealousy (or frustrated love or hatred), with the bourgeois passion greed significantly outdistancing all other drives.

The hero of the classical detective story, like that of its predecessors, matches analytical wit against criminal guile. The murderers have done everything possible to cover their tracks, and suspense reigns until they are discovered and proof of guilt has been presented. The key to this conventionalized system of crime and punishment is neither ethics, nor pity, nor understanding, but the formal proof of guilt, which will, in turn, lead to a verdict of 'guilty' by the jury. The abstract, rational character of the plot, the crime, and the exposure of the criminal make the classical detective story, even more than its nineteenth-century forerunners, the epitome of bourgeois rationality in literature. Formal logic rules supreme. Crime and its unmasking are like supply and demand in the market place: abstract absolute laws almost completely alienated from real human beings and the clashes of real human passions.

It is this that distinguishes the detective story from non-trivial literature dealing with crime. It is not the mystery of the criminal act (whodunit?) but the tragic ambiguity of human motivation and fate that lies at the centre of such works as Ricarda Huch's *Der Fall Deruga* or Dostoevsky's *Crime and Punishment*, not to mention *Macbeth* or *Oedipus Rex*. Real literature, like real art, reflects society as through the 'broken mirror' of the author's subjectivity, to repeat a formula of Trotsky's reiterated by Terry Eagleton. In *Trivialliteratur* that subjectivity is absent, and society is 'reflected' only in order to cater, for commercial purposes, to some supposed needs of the readers.

But here the similarity between the classical detective story and its original forebears stops. There are important differences between Sherlock Holmes, Inspector Lecoq, or Dr Thorndike on the one hand and Hercule Poirot, Lord Peter Wimsey, and Albert Campion on the other. In its effort to achieve unity of time, place and action, the classical detective story abandons the foggy streets of London and the contrasts of metropolitan Paris in favour of the drawing room and the English country house. Conan Doyle's London or Gaston Leroux's (not to mention Arsène Lupin's) Paris reflected (albeit in a simplified and increasingly conventional manner) the real struggle that the bourgeois industrialist, shopkeeper and banker had to wage to carve out places for themselves in the universal competition of rising bourgeois civilization.

In Agatha Christie's British country house, or Ellery Queen's or Rex Stout's American upper-class mansions, we see not a conquering but a stabilized bourgeoisie, one in which *rentiers* and not entrepreneurs call the tune. Indeed, the confinement of the setting of the classical detective story to the stable upper class itself frequently becomes formalized, as in Rex Stout's novels: Nero Wolfe charges astronomical fees, so the mysteries are generally those that affect rich bourgeois. The description of the upper-class milieu is sometimes spiced with humour and irony, as in the works of Dorothy Sayers and Rex Stout, and partially in those of Anthony Berkeley and A.A. Fair. But the domination of the upper-class setting and values is too obvious not to be emphasized.

Although the classical detective story is a highly formalized genre, the structural connection of that formalism to the substance of bourgeois society is not itself formal, but deeply rooted and thorough. The crimes of the drawing rooms, country houses, millionaires' mansions, and boards of directors' offices are marginal in society. They are exceptions, rather than the rule. The murderers of the first detective stories still had some relation to real criminals, with the 'dangerous' or 'criminal classes', with real crimes committed in the slums and red-light districts. The crimes of the classical detective story, on the other hand, become shadowy, abstract, and make-believe. It is precisely because the universe of the classical detective story is that of the triumphant *rentier* ruling class of the pre- and post-1914 period in the Anglo-Saxon countries (and to a far lesser extent in France; in the rest of the imperialist countries the species faded away after the first world war) that the treatment of crime can become so highly schematic, conventional and artificial.

In fact, it would not be an unreasonable exaggeration to maintain that the real problem of the classical detective novel is not crime at all – and certainly not violence or murder as such. It is rather death and mystery, the latter more than the former. Nor is this accidental. Mystery is the only irrational factor that bourgeois rationality cannot eliminate: the mystery of its own origins, the mystery of its own laws of motion, and most of all the mystery of its ultimate destiny. The self-confident Anglo-Saxon bourgeois of 1910, 1920, or even 1935 (despite the Depression), as embodied in the unflappable assurance of a Philo Vance or the unerring intellect of an Ellery Queen, relentlessly seeks to solve the Mystery of It All, peeling away layer after layer of false impressions, misleading clues and red herrings. Life and society are palimpsests that none but the Great Mind dare seek to read. Is that not, after all, what modern science, rising along with the bourgeoisie, seeks to achieve? But mystery always returns. Every hero has to go through the identical motions repeatedly, as each year brings its own crop of riddles –

each semester or quarter for the most prolific writers. Dickson Carr's hero Gideon Fell even specializes in mysteries in which what appears to be supernatural turns out in the end to be perfectly natural, accounted for by logical and scientific explanations.

In the classical detective story, the triumphant bourgeoisie celebrates the victory of its *ratio* over the forces of obscurity. But the victory is never final or complete. Yet another murderer, yet another bundle of contradictory clues, lurks around the corner. And as Dorothy Sayers's Lord Peter Wimsey exclaims in *Unnatural Death* (1927): 'Discovered murders are unsuccessful murders. The really successful ones are those which remain unknown.' (According to Sayers, in Britain in the 1920s only about 60 per cent of those responsible for deaths suspected to have been caused by foul play were brought to trial for murder.)

Finally, most of the famous heroes of the classical detective story were themselves members of the upper classes. Lord Peter Wimsey, Sir Henry Merrivale (said to have been physically patterned after Winston Churchill, no less, though before his moment of greatest fame), Albert Campion and Roderick Alleyn are scions of the aristocracy. Philo Vance, Ellery Queen, Nigel Strangeways, Hercule Poirot, and Nero Wolfe are rich eccentrics, genteel bourgeois of fortune; likewise Perry Mason, most of Anthony Berkeley's heroes, and Mr and Mrs North. In fact, in the entire list of the heroes of the classical detective story, the only exception would seem to be Charlie Chan. But then a Chinese police inspector in the 1920s could not have been part of the ruling class, could he?[1]

Granted, most of these detectives are bourgeois dilettantes and not really functioning capitalists, to use Marx's term. But again, that is typical of bourgeois society, which is based upon a functional division of labour within the ruling class. Making money, after all, is a full-time job in the competitive atmosphere of capitalism, and those who specialize in it have little time left over for other things. The job of trying to uncover the mystery of it all – like the task of conducting affairs of state or administering colonial peoples – is safely left to other, minor sectors of the class, at least as long as things remain fairly stable.

Robert Graves and Alan Hodge wrote:

> Low-brow reading was now dominated by the detective
> novel. A large number of writers made comfortable incomes
> from this fashion, and a curious situation arose. In Great
> Britain, though a few score murders and acts of grand larceny
> took place every year, not more than two or three of these had
> features in the least interesting to the criminologist as regards
> either motive or method; nor in any of these, did private
> detectives play a decisive part in bringing the culprits to
> justice – this was done by the competent routine procedure of
> the C.I.D. Yet from the middle of the twenties onwards,
> some thousands of detective novels were annually published,
> all of them concerned with extraordinary and baffling
> crimes, and only a very small number gave the police the least
> credit for the solution. These books were designed not as
> realistic accounts of crime, but as puzzles to test the readers'
> acuteness in following up disguised clues. It is safe to say that
> not one in a hundred showed any first-hand knowledge of the
> elements that comprised them – police organisation, the
> coroner's court, fingerprints, firearms, poison, the laws of
> evidence – and not one in a thousand had any verisimilitude.
> The most fanciful unprofessional stories (criminologically
> speaking) were the most popular. Detective novels, however,
> were no more intended to be judged by realistic standards
> than one would judge Watteau's shepherds and shepherd-
> esses in terms of contemporary sheep-farming. (pp.300-03)

But that is the whole point. Conventionalized and formalized
'trivial' literature, like conventionalized and formalized forms of
art in general, are not supposed to reflect reality at all. They are
intended to satisfy subjective needs, thus performing an objective
function: to reconcile the upset, bored and anxious individual
member of the middle class with the inevitability and permanence
of bourgeois society. The subjective need to be filled by the
classical detective story of the inter-war years was that of nostalgia.

For the mass of the petty bourgeoisie of the Anglo-Saxon

countries and of most of Europe, as well as for part of the more mellow sections of the ruling class, the first world war marked a watershed. In their minds it was linked with Paradise Lost: the end of stability, of the freedom to enjoy life at a leisurely pace and acceptable cost, of belief in an assured future and limitless progress. The war and its destruction, the millions killed, the ensuing revolutions, and the inflation, economic upheavals, and crises, meant the end for ever of that *douceur de vivre* which serious bourgeois authors as different as Marcel Proust, Stefan Zweig, John Galsworthy, and Scott Fitzgerald expressed with so much sensitivity. When the war ended and stability failed to return, the petty bourgeoisie, still essentially conservative, was consumed with nostalgia. The Republican administration in the United States, the Conservative Baldwin government in Britain, Poincaré in France, Stresemann and Brüning in Germany, relied upon that sentiment politically. The classical detective story was its pendant in the field of 'trivial' literature. The country-house and drawing-room settings of the novels, like Watteau's shepherds, are not a reflection of contemporary life, but a recollection of Paradise Lost. Through them, the Good Life of antebellum days was relived – in imagination if not in reality.

4. And back to the streets

The evolution of the crime story reflects the history of crime itself. With Prohibition in the United States, crime came of age, spreading from the fringes of bourgeois society into the very centre of things. Hijackings and gang warfare were no longer merely the stuff of popular literature, imbibed by readers with a pinch of excitement and fear; large numbers of citizens were confronted by them in daily life.

But the extension of crime in America that began with the 1920s, while launched by Prohibition, was by no means limited to violations of the law forbidding the manufacture and sale of alcoholic beverages. And when the Depression came, it gave a fresh and frightening impetus to crime of all sorts – bank robberies and the murders committed during them being the outstanding example.

With the quantitative extension of crime came a qualitative transformation of it. Organized crime came to dominate. There is a fascinating parallel between the laws governing the concentration and centralization of capital in general and the logic of organized crime's take-over of bootlegging, prostitution, gambling and the numbers game, and its achievement of dominance in cities like Las Vegas, Havana, and Hong Kong. With the expansion of activities, more capital was required for investment in trucks, weapons, killers, bribes for police and politicians, exploitation of foreign sources of supply (export of capital). The more capital available, the higher the profits and therefore the possibilities of reinvestment. Hence the extension of organization and the geographical spread.

Big fish swallow little ones, and large organizations easily triumph over individual entrepreneurs, among criminal gangs as among steel manufacturers. Even the rules of the game, the procedures, are strikingly alike: cut-throat competition, followed by cautious consultation (like the famous gangsters' conventions of May 1929 in Atlantic City and September 1931 in Chicago), leading to cartels (syndicates) that organize the division of territories and markets, and de facto fusions (mergers). Super-bosses (as anonymous as possible) impose discipline, and when the relationship of forces shifts, a renewal of competition occurs. Meyer Lansky, the financial genius of the crime syndicate, is said by French authors Jean-Michel Charlier and Jean Marcilly to have been inspired by the book *Making Profits*, by the Harvard economist William Taussig.

Organized crime, of course, predates Prohibition. Muckraker journalists had uncovered networks of graft and corruption linking the construction trade and public-works entrepreneurs to local and state politicians in many regions of the United States during the period after the Civil War. Friedrich Engels was only expressing an opinion widely shared by average American citizens when he wrote that the two-party system was no more than the means by which two gangs of thieves competed to plunder the public:

> It is well known how the Americans have been trying for
> thirty years to shake off this joke, which has become
> intolerable, and how in spite of it all they continue to sink
> ever deeper in this swamp of corruption. It is precisely in
> America that we see best how there takes place this process of
> the state power making itself independent in relation to
> society, whose mere instrument it was originally intended to
> be. Here there exists no dynasty, no nobility, no standing
> army, beyond the few men keeping watch on the Indians, no
> bureaucracy with permanent posts or the right to pensions.
> And nevertheless we find here two great gangs of political
> speculators, who alternately take possession of the state
> power and exploit it by the most corrupt means and for the
> most corrupt ends – and the nation is powerless against these
> two great cartels of politicians, who are ostensibly its
> servants, but in reality dominate and plunder it. (vol. 2,
> pp.483-84)

The importance of graft for individual politicians and police chiefs can be gauged by the millions of dollars involved. In 1924, the New York City chief of police, Joseph A. Warren, is said to have received $20,000 a week, while his successor, Grover A. Whalen, was taking in $50,000 from 1926 onwards. Hundreds, if not thousands, of lower-ranking cops were, of course, receiving smaller sums (see Charlier and Marcilly, p.75). One Hong Kong senior police officer is said to have received up to £9,000 a month in bribes ($150,000 a year); a detective, in the course of twelve years service in the Hong Kong police force, is reported to have amassed a fortune of 40 million Hong Kong dollars ($7 million) through bribes (see O'Callaghan, pp.82, 85). The Mafia itself – which originated in a legitimate political endeavour: to fight against the take-over and plunder of Sicily by the Bourbons – gradually expanded into import and manufacturing, illegal immigration, smuggling and so on. It is interesting to note that the Triads, the Chinese secret society, had a similarly political origin in the seventeenth-century struggle against the Manchu dynasty's conquest of China. The Chinese organization, like the Italian, was transplanted to American soil by immigration in the late nineteenth and early twentieth centuries.

The Triads never succeeded in organizing crime in the United States on a semi-monopolistic scale, because they failed to corner the mass market in forbidden alcohol and related products during the twenties. They later came into their own through the drug trade. Although the Mafia maintained its position as the dominant force in the American underworld until the late twenties, it never established a monopoly on bootlegging. The market was too broad, and the organization and capital required too enormous to be controlled by a narrowly based ethnic-centred group like the Sicilian Mafia. A wider amalgamation was needed, and it was brought about under the guidance of Lucky Luciano. It included the Mafia, embraced the whole of the United States, and began to expand abroad.

It was the constitution of that crime syndicate that marked the real coming of age of organized crime in bourgeois society. The US crime syndicate – aptly called the Organization – is but the prototype, and by no means the sole example. Japan, France,

Britain, Germany, Brazil, Argentina, and Turkey – to name just a few countries – each has an equivalent structure. While the Triads never attained that status in the United States, they did do so in pre-revolutionary China, at least in the largest cities, like Shanghai, and they now seem to be achieving it in Hong Kong, Singapore, and Taiwan. Little is known in the West about the Japanese crime syndicate called the Yakuza, said to have a yearly turnover of several billion dollars and to be divided into two warring factions, the Sumiyoshi Rengo, supposed to dominate Tokyo crime, and the Yamugushi Rengo, apparently controlling much of crime in western Japan. (*Atlanta Journal and Constitution*, 8 January 1984)

The coming of age of organized crime tolled the death knell of the drawing-room detective story. It is impossible to imagine Hercule Poirot, not to mention Lord Peter Wimsey or Father Brown, battling against the Mafia. Even the formidable Nero Wolfe takes fright when he finds himself confronting Zeck, the mysterious figure of organized crime. This is not to say that crime stories began to deal with the syndicate from the early thirties onwards; that would come later. But mass consciousness about the nature of criminal activities had caught up with violence of the St Valentine's Day type early enough to make drawing-room murders appear increasingly atypical, if not improbable.

This mass consciousness first came to the surface in the so-called pulp magazines, which developed more or less simultaneously with the rise of organized crime. Their prototype was the *Black Mask* series, founded in 1920 by two well-known American intellectuals, H. L. Mencken and George Jean Nathan, in an attempt to raise the money to finance their sophisticated, up-market magazine *Smart Set*. Several *Black Mask* collaborators later became famous, among them Erle Stanley Gardner and Dashiell Hammett.

The term *roman noir* has often been applied to post-war literature of the forties and fifties, said to have been initiated by Marcel Duhamel's *série noire* of crime thrillers. But this is inaccurate. The *roman noir* was actually born in the thirties, and grew out of the *Black Mask* tradition.

It was then that the first great revolution in the crime novel occurred. The two dominant figures of that revolution were

Dashiell Hammett and Raymond Chandler. Three other prominent names could perhaps be added: the Belgian Georges Simenon,
the French Léon Mallet, and the Canadian Ross Macdonald. But
Simenon's hero Inspector Maigret already represents yet another
development: the take-over from the private eye by the regular
police. And although Ross Macdonalds' Lew Archer is still very
much a private eye, he comes too late to be considered as part of the
turn that occurred in the thirties. Léon Malet's hero, Nestor
Burma, comes closest to the Hammett-Chandler pattern.

In his essay 'The Simple Art of Murder', Raymond Chandler
actually theorized the turn, and dated it as beginning with
Hammett's work. It was an abrupt break with the gentility of the
classical detective story, especially with crime based on individual
psychological motives like greed and revenge. Social corruption,
especially among the rich, now moves into the centre of the plots,
along with brutality, a reflection of both the change in bourgeois
values brought about by the first world war and the impact of
organized gangsterism.

But although the change in surroundings and atmosphere is real
enough, there remains an unmistakable continuity with the private
detectives of the traditional sort, with Sherlock Holmes, Lord
Peter Wimsey, Albert Campion, Philo Vance, Ellery Queen and
Nero Wolfe: the romantic pursuit of truth and justice for their own
sake. Sam Spade, Philip Marlowe, Nestor Burma, and Lew Archer
may seem hard-boiled characters cynically devoid of any illusions
in the existing social order. But at bottom they are still
sentimentalists, suckers for damsels in distress, for the weak
confronting the strong. In a classic passage of 'The Simple Art of
Murder' Chandler himself describes this combination of cynicism
and romanticism:

> Down these mean streets a man must go who is neither
> tarnished nor afraid. The detective in this kind of story must
> be such a man. He is the hero, he is everything. He must be a
> complete man and a common man and yet an unusual man.
> He must be, to use a rather weathered phrase, a man of
> honour, by instinct, by inevitability, without thought of it,
> and certainly without saying it.

It is not difficult to detect the naivety of that portrait. The notion of an individual confrontation with organized crime, Don Quixote style, has not a little of the adolescent fantasy about it, and nothing to do with the social reality of the twenties and thirties. For the exploits of Sam Spade, Philip Marlowe and Lew Archer to be credible, they must be dealing ultimately with petty criminals. The culprit may be a local tycoon, Hollywood star or rich adventurer instead of a pathetic butler in a British country house or a young bounder out to snag an inheritance before uncle changes his will, but is nonetheless a criminal who wields only limited clout – not a powerful Mafia-style leader, nor even a large corporation.

The hard-boiled cynical sentimentalist will track these criminals down by obstinate questioning and constant moves from place to place, not through the painstaking analysis of clues and related analytical reasoning. The prominence of this process of *tracking down* is itself a clue to the shift in bourgeois values reflected in the 'revolution' of the classical detective story. It is linked to another change. Hard-boiled private eyes, while still individualists *par excellence*, are no longer eccentric or rich dilettantes. Detecting is their business, providing them with a livelihood, most often a modest one. They operate, not from home, but from an office, and often have the support of a nascent organization, sometimes a partner, sometimes a secretary. They mark a transitional stage between detecting as a fine art and as a large-scale organized profession.

Raymond Chandler (*The Big Sleep*, 1939; *Farewell, My Lovely*, 1940) should not be judged solely in the light of his personal itinerary: from English public school, to civil service, to the US oil business, to socially critical writing, to Hollywood and capitulation to McCarthyism. His creative contribution to literature in general and to the crime novel in particular cannot be denied. But because his writing is motivated by contempt for big-city corruption, its ideological slant has often been misunderstood. It is only the *local*, never the national, power structure that is denounced in Chandler's works. (This same is true, incidentally, of John D. Macdonald's more socially critical efforts, as in his novel *Condominium*, 1977.) His ideology is still basically bourgeois, as Stephen Knight has correctly emphasized:

In all the novels it is clear enough that the scene dominates the structure, rather than fitting the hero into a worked out sequence of events as Christie offered, working back from her ending. Chandler's own habit of working on half-sheets of paper was intended to sharpen his small-scale focus, making overall connections less evident and enabling him to concentrate his rewriting on detailed matters rather than plot-revision. Chandler remarked, only half in fun, that when he was in doubt he had a man come through the door with a gun in his hand.

The scenes are controlled by Marlowe's scrutiny of the characters, not by the characters themselves, and his need to react in full negative detail against others is what runs away with the scenes. Chandler was not willing to curtail this development for the sake of a shapely plot, because it was central to his meaning; he was writing *personalized adventures of a hero*, not plots which created a sharply focused problem or a pattern of social reality. (p.129, emphasis added)

Social reality and criticism are far stronger in Chandler's follower, the most prolific representative of the creators of tough-guy private eyes, Ross Macdonald. A Canadian educated in his own country, Macdonald (*The Moving Target*, 1949; *The Chill*, 1964; *The Far Side of the Dollar*, 1965) is more overtly anti-capitalist than Chandler, although his hero, Lew Archer, is a milder fellow than Chandler's Philip Marlowe: 'I'm a detective. A kind of poor-man's sociologist.' 'The whole valley spread out below, you can imagine it's a promised land. Maybe it is for a few. But for every air-conditioned ranch house with ts swimming pool and private landing-strip, there are dozens of tin-sided shacks and broken-down trailers where lost tribes of migrant workers live.'

Ross Macdonald's hard-boiled Lew Archer nearly closes the circle. He is almost entirely a *product of events*. Most of his cases involve disappearances, and when he tracks down his culprits, he is impelled by circumstance, as his personal initiative disappears too.

The revolution in setting and *modus operandi* was accompanied by a revolution in tone and language. The leisurely, sometimes even slovenly style of Agatha Christie, and the arrogant wittiness of

Dorothy Sayers or S.S. Van Dine, with its in-jokes and pseudo-sophistication, gives way to economy of means. Direct, hard-hitting dialogue becomes the real craft, and its handling is often masterly. One Nobel Prize winner, André Gide, had this to say (in his *Journals* entry of 16 March 1943) about Dashiell Hammett, comparing him to two other Nobel Prize winners:

> Read with very keen interest (and why not dare to say admiration) *The Maltese Falcon*, by Dashiell Hammett (1930), by whom I already read last summer, but in translation, the amazing *Red Harvest* (1929), far superior to the *Falcon*, to *The Thin Man* (1934), and to a fourth novel, obviously written on order, the title of which escapes me. In English, or at least in American, many subtleties of the dialogue escape me, but in *Red Harvest* the dialogues, written in a masterful way, are such as to give pointers to Hemingway or even to Faulkner, and the entire narrative is ordered with skill and an implacable cynicism. In that very special type of thing it is, I really believe, it is the most remarkable I have read.

Two precursors should be mentioned: Donald Henderson Clarke (*Louis Beretti: The Story of a Gunman*, 1929) and William Riley Burnett (*Little Caesar*, 1929), both inspired by the stories of real gangsters. A later book by Burnett, *High Sierra*, said by Javier Coma (p.43), to have been inspired by the Dillinger case, contains what could well be called a gangster's philosophy (an echo of which would appear, much later, in Mario Puzo's *The Godfather*): 'Look, in this country only a few have all the money. Millions don't have enough to eat, not because there isn't enough, but because they don't have the money. Others do. Okay, why don't the ones without money get together and get their hands on it?' (Translated from Coma's book, where it is quoted in Spanish.) But the gangster Roy Erle, who speaks these words for Burnett, goes in for individual and not collective expropriation. That doesn't change the system of haves and have-nots, just the list of the haves.

In the hard-boiled private detective story, the revolution in subject, setting, style and solution can also be traced back to technological innovations. What photography and railways were to the original 'whodunit', the movies and the automobile are to the *roman noir*.

Tracking down criminals instead of examining clues, substituting a string of scenes to a well-constructed plot, moving faster and faster from scene to scene, what is the *roman noir* but the motion picture erupting into popular literature, as the thriller later erupted into the movies by way of the gangster story first, the suspense story later? George Raft leads to Philip Marlowe who will lead to Humphrey Bogart and to Hitchcock.

As Mary McCarthy wrote (*New York Times Book Review*, April 1984) of the novelist Joan Didion:

> Like the camera, this mental apparatus does not think, but projects images, very haunting and troubling ones for the most part, precisely because they are mute. Even when sonorized, as has happened here, they remain silent and somewhat frightening in their stunned aversion from thought.

5. The ideology of the detective story

Preoccupation with death is as old as humanity. Death, like labour, is our inevitable fate. But it is a natural fatality mediated by social conditions determined by particular socio-economic structures. The causes of death, and its moment, depend upon social conditions to a large extent. Infant mortality and life expectancy have varied widely throughout history, and so have ideas about death. The social history of death is a precious source of information about the social history of life.

The development of commodity production and the emergence of generalized commodity production, or capitalism, have profoundly altered attitudes toward death. In primitive societies and in class societies still based essentially on the production of use-values, death is seen as a result of nature, as something for which people have to prepare themselves, aided by the attention of their families and the social groups within which they are integrated. Hence respect for elders and the culture of ancestors, which is part of an attempt to accept death as a natural end of life.

In societies based upon the production and circulation of exchange-values, competition between individuals reigns supreme. People are judged not for the maturity of their experience or for their strength of character, but for their performance in the rat race. Older people are therefore considered a burden, increasingly useless, inasmuch as they do not hold jobs and earn money. Protection of the old becomes increasingly de-personalized, anonymous, and taken over by bureaucratic apparatuses.

Because of the changed fate of the elderly, the altered relation between the individual and the community, and the absolute rule of value and money, capital and wealth, the alienated human being in bourgeois society is obsessed with the integrity of the body, indispensable instrument of labour and earning. Hence a much greater obsession with death. Hence also the view that death is a catastrophic accident and not an inevitable conclusion of life. Indeed, accidents are a rising cause of death statistically: road accidents, wars, the 'diseases of civilization'. Accidental death has taken the place of ontological death in the bourgeois consciousness of death, and certainly in the ideology of death.[1]

Boileau and Narcejac maintain that fear is at the root of the ideology of the detective novel. But fear, in particular fear of death, is as old as humanity. It cannot explain why the crime story did not originate in the fifth century BC or during the Renaissance. The crime story requires a particular kind of fear of death, one that clearly has its roots in the conditions of bourgeois society. Obsession with death seen as an accident leads to obsession with violent death, and hence to obsession with murder, with crime.

Traditionally, preoccupation with death treats it as an anthropological question (magic, theology, philosophy) or as an individual tragedy (institutionalized religion, literature, psychology). With the advent of the detective story as a specific literary genre, a significant break in that tradition occurs. Death – and more particularly murder – is at the very centre of the crime story. There is hardly one without violent death. (The novels of Paul Erdman are an interesting exception.) But death in the crime story is not treated as a human fate, or as a tragedy. It becomes an object of enquiry. It is not lived, suffered, feared or fought against. It becomes a corpse to be dissected, a thing to be analyzed. Reification of death is at the very heart of the crime story.

This phenomenon of the reification of death in the crime story amounts to the replacement of preoccupation with human destiny by preoccupation with crime. And as I mentioned earlier, this is the line that divides the murders occurring in great literature – from Sophocles to Shakespeare, Stendhal, Goethe, Dostoevsky, Dreiser – from those occurring in crime stories. Preoccupation with crime, however, is preoccupation with certain objective rules, with law and order, with *individual* security, the safety of someone's (or some family's) personal fate in a limited portion of life (by definition, subjects like wars, revolutions and depressions fall outside the purview of this sort of security). Preoccupation with crime and personal security leads inevitably to a Manichaean polarization. Personal security is good by definition; an attack against it is evil by nature. Psychological analysis, the complexity and ambiguity of human motives and behaviour, has no place within that Manichaeanism. The crime story is based upon the mechanical, formal division of the characters into two camps: the bad (the criminals) and the good (the detective and the more or less inefficient police).

The extreme polarization of the universe of the crime story, however, is accompanied by a de-personalization of good and evil, one that is part and parcel of the de-humanization of death. Good and evil are not embodied in real human beings, in real complex personalities. There is no battle of passions and wills, only a clash of wits, analytical as opposed to precautionary cleverness. Clues have to be *discovered* because tracks have been *covered*. Instead of human conflict, there is competition between abstract intelligences. This competition is like that of the market-place, where what is involved is a struggle over cost-prices and sales-prices, and not between complex human beings. That reification of conflict reflects the reification of death as a reification of human fate.

Of course, such reification is not purely negative. In feudal and despotic societies, torture was the main means of 'proving' crimes and unmasking criminals. Innocents died under torture in horrible pain. By formalizing the process of proof-gathering, submitting it to rules based on the principles of bourgeois values, nineteenth-century criminal justice meant a historical step forward for human liberty, however limited and contradictory a step it may have been. To characterize that advance as hypocritical is to close one's eyes to the obvious fact that the elimination of torture is a key conquest of the bourgeois-democratic revolution, one that socialists do not reject but must defend and integrate into the socialist revolution and the building of socialism.

By replacing scholastic disputes with clue-gathering in the process of crime-detection, by replacing confessions extracted under torture with formalized proof acceptable in court as the basis of a verdict of guilty, science at least partially supplants magic, rationality at least partially supplants irrationality. In that sense, as

Ernst Bloch has pointed out, the detective story reflects and summarizes the historical progress won by the revolutionary bourgeoisie, for obvious reasons of self-defence and self-interest.

But rationality and rationalism are not identical. Reified rationality is incompletely and therefore insufficiently rational. It cannot grasp or explain the human condition in its totality, but artificially breaks it up into separate compartments: economic, political (citizen), cultural, sexual, moral, psychological, religious. Criminals are the products of their drives, the heroes products of their search for justice (or for order). Within such a formalized context, it is impossible to understand, or even to pose, the way the criminal and detective alike, along with crime and justice, prison and property, are products of the same society, of a specific stage of social development. Crime and the detecting of crime are not only reified, but also made banal and without problems. They are taken for granted, outside the specific social context and concrete historical development that have created them.

Bourgeois rationalism is always a combination of rationality and irrationality, and it produces a growing trend toward overall irrationality. That is why the detective story, while placing analytical intelligence and scientific clue-gathering at the heart of crime detection, often resorts to blind passions, crazy plots, and references to magic, if not to clinical madness, in order to 'explain' why criminals commit crimes. Conan Doyle himself symbolizes that contradiction by his rising concern for the supernatural, which moved him, late in life, to write a book seeking to prove the existence of fairies. Even if individual passion were the dominant motive for crime, there would still be the question of why a given social context produces more and more madness while another does not – a question the classical detective story never raises.

The very structure of the classical detective novel reflects this combination. As Professor Dresden pointed out in the Dutch study *Marionettenspel met de Dood,* such a novel moves at two levels of reality simultaneously. On the one hand, everything must look as real and matter-of-fact as possible. Exact time is always mentioned, precise locations offered, sometimes complete with maps and other sketches. The actions of the characters are described in the most minute detail, as are their clothes and physical appearance. At the same time, everything is shrouded in ambiguity and mystery. Sinister shadows lurk in the background. People are not what they seem. Unreality constantly takes over from reality. Simenon brings out this contrast – and combination – in two telling sentences: 'Maigret watched the passers-by and told himself that Paris was peopled by mysterious and elusive beings that you come across only rarely, in the course of some tragedy.' 'It was good to come back to the voice of Mrs Maigret, to the smell of the flat, with the furniture and objects in their place.'

Disorder being brought into order, order falling back into disorder; irrationality upsetting rationality, rationality restored after irrational upheavals: that is what the ideology of the crime novel is all about.

It is no accident that this classical detective story developed primarily in the Anglo-Saxon countries. One of the central characteristics of the prevailing ideology in Britain and the United States during the latter half of the nineteenth century and the early years of the twentieth was the absence, or at least extreme debility, of concepts of class struggle as tools for the interpretation of social phenomena. (In Britain, this represented a regression compared with earlier periods.) This reflected the stability of bourgeois society and the self-confidence of the ruling class. The intelligentsia in general, and authors of books in particular, whether socially critical or conservative, assumed that this stability was a fact of life.

In these circumstances, it was natural for them to assimilate revolt against the social order into criminal activity, to identify the rebellious proletariat with the 'criminal classes' (an expression that crops up repeatedly in popular Anglo-Saxon detective stories). What began as natural soon acquired a social function, and an effective one at that. In France, by contrast, although academics writing for an exclusively bourgeois audience might use such a phrase, the lower-middle classes and literate workers, who made up the mass audience of the popular novel, would certainly not have accepted such notions after experiences like the 1848 revolution or the Paris Commune. Just because the class struggle was sharper and more politicized in France than in the Anglo-Saxon countries, it was far more difficult, and therefore far less effective and thus less widely practised, to criminalize class conflict or to subsume it under individual conflicts.

It is interesting to note that in Germany and Japan 'serious' detective stories began to sink national roots only after the second world war (with authors such as Hansjörg Martin, Thomas Andresen, Friedhelm Werremaier, Richard Hey, Irène Rodrian, and Ky), although J.D.H. Temme had written many kinds of crime stories in the 1860s.[2] Only at that point in history bourgeois ideology in its purest sense became all-pervasive. But in both cases, momentous social upheavals – war, defeat, foreign occupation and spectacular economic expansion in its wake – made it impossible to write stories with an atmosphere of secular order and normality. The context of crime is wealth and business, sometimes with a modestly critical social dimension.

Significantly, the criminals in most of these novels are themselves entrepreneurs and corporation managers. Their motive is nearly always greed or the pressure of financial difficulties.

A substantial anthology of Latin American mystery stories, edited by Donald Yates, *Latin Blood: The Best Crime and Detective Stories of South America*, was published in 1972. The Dutch author Erik Lankester has doubled the input in his *Zuidamerikaanse Misdaadverhalen* (1982), including such famous writers as Borges, Cortazar, Gabriel Garcia Marquez, Ben Traven, who have all dabbled in crime stories.

While the criminalization of the lower classes is a special feature of the more trivial Anglo-Saxon detective novels, it is not unusual to find middle-class, and even wealthy, murderers in the classical crime stories of the twenties and thirties (Agatha Christie's novels, for example). The key point is not the class origin of the murderer, but his presentation as a social misfit, a 'bounder' who violates the norms of the ruling class and must be punished for that very reason.

Likewise, it is only partially correct to assimilate the British and American traditions of the mystery novel. In Britain, rising capitalism was integrated with a consolidated state, the product of a protracted historical development and combined, as concerns the social superstructure, with many remnants of semi-feudal super-structure. Hence the general atmosphere of class divisions accepted by consensus in the classical British detective story, an acceptance expressed even at the level of language. Violence, absent from the centre of the social scene, is pushed to the periphery (the colonies, Ireland, working-class slums). The state is relatively weak, the London police unarmed, because of the apparent stability of society. To some extent, this was a false impression, but it did determine the way ruling ideology reflected British reality, and thus the framework within which the detective novel developed in Britain.

When the centre of world capitalism shifted from Britain to the United States, the international system had already ceased expanding and had begun its decline, although US capitalism continued to expand. The growth of American capitalism was therefore accompanied by declining faith in bourgeois values, although up to 1929, if not 1945, they remained more widely accepted in American society than in less stable and wealthy capitalist countries.

But this decline was combined with a different historical tradition, a different form of integration of the capitalist order and the bourgeois state. Just because American capitalism was the 'purest' in the world (once slavery was abolished), with no semi-feudal remnants and no hierarchical order of pre-capitalist origin, prevailing social values were less deeply anchored in tradition and less thoroughly internalized by the population. The bourgeoisie was much less respectful of its own state.

Corruption, violence, and crime were evident not only in the periphery of American society, but in its very centre. Where the British civil service was a genuine servant of bourgeois society and the successful British politician was seen as a public sage, the American civil service was regarded as virtually useless throughout the nineteenth century, and successful politicians were seen as crooks. From the outset, then, the American crime story presented crime as far more completely integrated into society as a whole than the British did.

The theme is still the clash between individual interests and passions, but the events of the novels are less artificial, less tangential to the bourgeois order as a whole, than in the British mystery story. Passion, greed, power, envy, jealousy and property do not merely set individual against individual, but increasingly involve conflicts between individuals and groups or families, and even revolts against class conformism. Crime becomes a means by which to climb the social ladder, or to remain a capitalist despite financial disasters. It is the road from threatened hell to paradise regained. It is the nightmare that stalks the American dream as the shadow stalks the body. The differences between Dashiell Hammett, Raymond Chandler, Ross Macdonald and even Ellery Queen on the one hand and Agatha Christie, Dorothy Sayers, Anthony Berkeley and John Dickson Carr on the other originate in this specificity of bourgeois society in the United States.

Nevertheless, the common ideology of the original and classical detective story in Britain, the United States, and the countries of the European continent remains quintessentially bourgeois. Reified death; formalized crime-detection oriented toward proof acceptable in courts of justice operating according to strictly defined rules; the pursuit of the criminal by the hero depicted as a battle between brains; human beings reduced to 'pure' analytical intelligence; partial fragmented rationality elevated to the status of an absolute guiding principle of human behaviour; individual conflicts used as a generalized substitute for conflicts between social groups and layers – all this is bourgeois ideology *par excellence*, a striking synthesis of human alienation in bourgeois society.

It plays a powerful integrative role among all but extremely critical and sophisticated readers. It suggests to them that individual passions, drives, and greed, and the social order itself – bourgeois society – have to be accepted as such regardless of shortcomings and injustices, and that those who catch criminals and deliver them to law-enforcement agencies, the courts, and the gallows or electric chair are serving the interests of the immense majority of the citizenry. The class nature of the state, property, law and justice remains completely obscured. Total irrationality combined with partial rationality, condensed expression of bourgeois alienation, rules supreme. The detective story is the realm of the happy ending. The criminal is always caught. Justice is always done. Crime never pays. Bourgeois legality, bourgeois values, bourgeois society, always triumph in the end. It is soothing, socially integrating literature, despite its concern with crime, violence and murder.

S. Vestdijk has called attention to the similarities and dissimilarities of the detective story and the game of chess. In both cases we have a limited number of players and strictly conventional rules, which are mechanical and purely rational in nature; both are deterministic, each move determined by the previous ones and leading to the next. But the differences are no less striking. In chess, the winner is the one who really manifests superior rational skill and memory (although capacity for concentration and absence of nervous over-reaction and anxiety also play a role in determining the winner). In the classical detective story, on the other hand, the winner is predetermined by the author. Like the hunted fox, the criminal never wins. It is not fair play, but fake play under the guise of fair play. It is a game with loaded dice. Bourgeois rationality is a cheater's rationality. The 'best man' never wins; the richest does. Private property, law and order, must triumph, regardless of the cost in human life and misery. For the 'survival of the fittest' (meaning the richest) to be disguised as fair play, the detective must be a super-brain, and the predetermined winner must appear as the best player.

Many crime-story writers began as 'mechanical writers' churning the stuff out for a pittance paid by pulp magazines. But the inner drive that moved them to write was anything but mechanical. In his biography of the creator of Sherlock Holmes, *Portrait of an Artist: Conan Doyle*, Julian Symons points out that the decent, law-abiding, patriotic, and typically Victorian bourgeois Conan Doyle invented a hero with quite the opposite personality: a brainy, Bohemian, violin-playing drug addict. He suggests that there were really two Conan Doyles: 'Behind the beefy face and rampant moustaches lurked another figure, hurt, perplexed and uncomforting.'

Edgar Allan Poe's early writing was dominated by his tormented anxiety and hallucinations, which prevented him from conducting a normal life and earning a normal living. Suddenly he got a job as editor of the popular journal *Graham's* in Philadelphia. For the only time of his life he was better off. He desperately wanted to keep that job. Was that the drive that transformed his gothic-romantic writing into the pure rationalism of *The Murders in the Rue Morgue*? This is at least the hypothesis of the literary historian Howard Haycraft in *The Life and Times of the Detective Story*. We see the parallel with the older Thomas De Quincey, whose hallucinations are twisted into reasonable logic and persiflage in his *Murder considered as one of the Fine Arts*.

In James Brabazon's biography of Dorothy Sayers, we learn of an obviously frustrated woman unable to have a normal relationship with a man of her own intellectual and moral standard and therefore projecting herself (Miss Harriet) and her fantasy Ideal Companion (Lord Peter Wimsey) into her books.

The case of Georges Simenon is even clearer. He has said that he was very religious up to the age of 13, even wanting to become a priest. Then, with his first sexual encounter, 'I saw that all that about guilt and sin was nonsense. I found out that all the sins I'd heard about were not sins at all.' (Interview in *The Sunday Times*, 16 May 1982.) When we read his poignant autobiography, *Mémoires Intimes*, we discover a deeply unhappy and guilt-ridden man. He boasts of having slept with ten thousand women, eight thousand of them prostitutes, but he has obviously been unable to establish real human relationships in the first place with women. ('The more ordinary a woman is, the more one can consider her as "woman", the more the act takes on significance'.) He is aware of having made his family deeply unhappy by his extravagance, drunkenness, and egoism, and he feels at least some guilt for the suicide of his daughter Marie-Jo.

Yet Inspector Maigret is the most ordinary of petty-bourgeois citizens, happy to return to his wife after a fair day's work for a fair day's pay, someone who would never dream of visiting a prostitute, let alone thousands of them. The life the author believes he would like to have lived is in his books. But how sincere is that belief? For after he had made some money (not necessarily millions), he did, after all, have a choice. And he was weak enough to choose wrongly, not only from the point of view of social morality, but also from the point of view of personal happiness. As he himself explained to the Paris daily *Le Monde* (13 November 1981): 'It's life that keeps me going ... I have seen misery close up, in slums throughout the world. I have seen the rich, and participated in their orgies.' But that was not really unavoidable, was it? It was a result of uncontrolled drives, which he continued to suffer, for which he felt deep guilt, and which he tried to sublimate in his books.

Graham Greene is the writer most conscious of the motives that make him write. As the conservative German historian Joachim Fest pointed out, (*Frankfurter Allgemeine Zeitung*, 10 April 1982), behind his books stands 'the need to escape the tedium of life, the monotony suffered as pain, and to escape it through experience of fear and of extreme risk'.[4] Here we find escapist literature, which helps the reader to endure the ills of bourgeois society, corresponding to the author's own need to escape, both through actual life (Greene's travelling and spying adventures) and through his writings. In his autobiography *Ways of Escape*, Greene writes: 'Sometimes I ask myself how all those who cannot write, compose, or paint are capable of escaping the absurdity, the sadness, and the panic fear which characterise the human condition.'

Adam Hall makes his hero Quiller, the technocratic spy, into a faceless operative like those employed by a great corporation, institution or government. He draws a picture of total alienation. Reading his speech to a potential recruit, we are left with the question: is this only Quiller's universe, or does it reflect the author's own inner despair?

> You've got to learn to cross the line and live your life outside society [!], shut yourself away from people, cut yourself off. Values are different out there. Let a man show friendship for you and you've got to deny him, mistrust him, suspect him, and nine times out of ten you'll be wrong but it's the tenth time that'll save you from a dirty death in a cheap hotel because you'd opened the door to a man you thought was a friend. Out there you'll be alone and you'll have no one you can trust, not even the people who are running you. Not even me. If you make the wrong kind of mistake at the wrong time in the wrong place, and it looks like you're fouling up the mission or exposing the Bureau, they'll throw you to the dogs. And so will I.

We've come a long way from the famous Raymond Chandler

formula about the quality of the lone detective walking down the streets.

Umberto Eco, who became interested in the crime novel through semiotics, tries to throw more light on his own inner motives for writing the famous detective story *The Name of the Rose*. He actually suggests that he was moved by the desire to murder a monk, which seized him in March 1978 (precisely!). Indeed, if it would be so easy to psychoanalyze oneself, a whole profession would soon be out of business.

Jack London provides the most fascinating and moving of cases. On the eve of his tragic suicide in 1916 he had almost finished one of the most amazing crime stories of all time. *Assassination Bureau Ltd* is the only truly philosophical crime novel. It is a battle of wits between two individuals who represent opposite trends in philosophy and in the radical movement. One embodies the attempt to eliminate social evil by the murder of evil individuals; the other one looks for a solution to the social question through self-organization and self-emancipation of the oppressed.

London starts from that elementary debate between the Nietzschean organizer of the Assassination Bureau and his Marxist nemesis (who is also the lover of the murderer's daughter) and proceeds to peel off layer after layer of subtle analysis. The head of the Assassination Bureau makes fun of the inefficiency of the traditional anarcho-terrorists. He actually tries to build a 'perfect organization' and in so doing comes strikingly close to becoming a Zinovievist ideological forerunner of Stalin. Some of his philosopher-murderers stick to rigid moral principles which they refuse to violate, even if it costs them their lives; but at the same time they murder for money. The Marxist hero, on the other hand, is somewhat like an anti-hero – a rich individualist who ends up by destroying the Assassination Bureau's chief while desperately trying to save him. He is unable to formulate or see through his own motives except that of general respect for the sanctity of human life, though that does not prevent him from killing a dozen people! But more than the fanatically principled assassin, it is he who is the genuine idealist and who is completely uninterested in money.

All the debates, adventures and increasing suspense of this

significant novel take place against the background of Jack London's premonition of the decline of capitalism into barbarism, his hatred of exploitation and injustice, his abhorrence of war and his identification with the 'people of the abyss', which makes him, in Trotsky's eyes, one of the greatest revolutionary thinkers of this century. But these agonizing reappraisals also reflect London's torment which in the end led to his suicide. He was unable to decide on a political course of action; he failed to live in conformity with his own convictions; and his desperate quest for personal happiness, which he so movingly projects onto several of his novels' heroes, also ended in failure.

6. From organized crime to organized detection

With the advent of organized crime on a large scale, a commensurate change in the detection and combating of crime in real life had to occur. During the thirties, the law-enforcement establishment grew massively throughout the Western world. A similar development in literature dealing with crime was inevitable too. With the late thirties and early forties, the private detective is on the wane, being ousted by the police officer supported by wide-ranging organization. A new type of crime story was born, the 'police procedural'.

Charlie Chan, Inspector Maigret, and Ellery Queen are typical transitional figures. Although he is in the police in Hawaii, Charlie Chan has little or no actual support from his office. In effect, he alone pits his wits against the murderer's. Although Inspector Maigret does get some aid from his department, it is a far cry from an organization relying on extensive technical expertise. Ellery Queen co-operates with his father, a police inspector, and thus occasionally is able to draw upon police resources. But he remains essentially a lone-wolf analyst of the classical detective story type. The real sign of police ascendancy in the crime story is the replacement of individual analysis by organizational resources as the main means of tracking down the criminal.

Police officers could become the heroes of crime stories because there had been a change in bourgeois values as reflected in that literary genre. The post-world-war-one period, with its intensification of class struggle, saw a change in the attitude of the upper class towards the permanent state apparatus, to which it had been hostile during the nineteenth century. No longer considered a necessary evil, the police came to be seen as the embodiment of social good in the eyes of the bourgeoisie. Police officers could thus become the heroes of detective stories, allowing for the inevitable time lag.

The transition of the police from objects of faint contempt to heroes was also facilitated by the fact that not all police officers are plebeians: some can be recruited from the upper class, or even the gentry, as exemplified by Ngaio Marsh's Roderick Alleyn. This change in recruitment occurred in reality as well, a reflection of the growth of the police apparatus, its increasingly hierarchical structure, and the need for the police hierarchy to dovetail the social hierarchy itself.

An additional explanation for the rising star of the police in the crime story is the need to legitimize them in the eyes of the public. The police officer is no longer merely the defender of law and order at the most vulgar level, the guardian of private property against burglars and petty thieves, but is increasingly the defender of order at the most exalted level: the defence of private property as an institution. The latter, threatened by war, crisis, and revolution, is no longer reproduced automatically by market forces but must be upheld by a permanent apparatus of repression.

Finally, the dimensions assumed by organized crime made new methods of law enforcement imperative not only in reality but also in literature. It is not possible for a single genius to solve fifty murders simultaneously, like a chess master playing against fifty amateurs at once. Nor is it possible to beat the Mafia by sheer wits. What is required is the establishment and growth of ever larger crime-detecting machines, using all the techniques of contemporary science and organized administration.

These techniques are deployed in autonomous branches of the police department, combining the advantages of division of labour and centralization of the results of that labour. Forensic medicine, increasingly sophisticated, facilitates the determination of the cause and time of death. Laboratories specialize in identifying suspects through the analysis of blood stains, dust particles, or hairs found on the victims or on their own clothes.

In his novel *The First Circle*, Solzhenitsyn has expert convicts working on an NKVD project of identifying human voices and codifying the information as the Bertillon system classifies fingerprints, enabling the police to centralize information about tens of millions of individuals the world over. The French government under Giscard d'Estaing had initiated a plan to establish computer records such that every inhabitant of the country would have a file centralizing information ranging from date of birth to school and army records, successive addresses, tax payments, police arrests and so on.

Besides this mass of scientific resources, there is the obstinate, routine plodding of hundreds, even thousands, of police ready to deploy infinite patience and endure unending boredom in tailing suspects, tracking down clues, staking out promising locations – not to mention legal and pseudo-legal electronic eavesdropping.

Embryonic samples of these techniques, of course, can be found in the activities of Sherlock Holmes and in the novels of R. Austin Freeman – but they are of necessity embryonic, secondary and haphazard. They are the home-made tools of a craft, not the departments of a modern factory. When the police officer bearing the force of an entire police organization supplants the prima donna hero of the classical detective story, crime detection comes of age as a modern scientific business enterprise, just as contemporary crime comes of age when corporation-like crime syndicates supplant individual criminals and petty street-gangs. A whole variety of police inspectors emerge as heroes, with a tantalizing range of idiosyncrasies, tastes, and psychological inclinations.

The real precursor is probably Freeman Wills Crofts's Inspector French, who brings all of police resources to bear in literary detecting. Together with G.D.H. Cole's Superintendent Henry Wilson and John Dickson Carr's Judge Bencolin and Superintendent Hadley, he slightly antedates the classical series of police-inspector heroes, who include, above all, Ngaio Marsh's Inspector Roderick Alleyn, Stanislaw-André Steeman's Commissioner Wenceslav Vorobeitchek, Claude Aveline's Commissioner Belot, Arthur W. Upfield's Inspector Napoleon Bonaparte, Ruth Bendell's Chief Inspector Reginald Wexford, Josephine Tey's Inspector Alan Grant, John Creasey's Inspector Roger West and Commander George Gideon, Ed McBain's team of detectives of the

87th Precinct, H.R.F. Keeting's Inspector Ghote, John Ball's Virgil Tibbs, R.L. Fisk's Brazilian detective Captain José Da Silva, Friedrich Dürrenmatt's Swiss Inspector Bärlach, Nicholas Freeling's Amsterdam Commissioner Van der Valk (and later his wife), Sjöwall and Wahö's Stockholm Commissioner Martin Beck, and Chester Himes's Harlem cops, Coffin Ed Johnson and Grave Digger Jones. Of late, one may add Lawrence Sanders's New York Chief of Detectives Edward Delaney and P.D. James's Scotland Yard Commander Adam Dalgliesh, both of whom are supposed to be portraits of real police chiefs.

Each of these police characters develops the crime novel in a given direction. Roderick Alleyn and Alan Grant are closest to the classical heroes. Although they enjoy the aid of the police department, their manner of operation is not very different from that of Charlie Chan, Philo Vance, Ellery Queen, or even Perry Mason and Nero Wolfe.

Van der Valk, Martin Beck, Wenceslas and Bärlach are closer to Maigret. Granted, they are backed up by far more legwork than is Simenon's hero. But in the end, they rely on psychological analysis, atmosphere, and their understanding of the people surrounding the crime. Intuition and feeling more than cold interpretation of clues guide them to their solutions.

Inspectors Ghote, West and Gideon, Tibbs, Da Silva, Commander Adam Dalgliesh, and above all the 87th Precinct team and Chief Delaney seem closer to actual police detectives, concentrating on routine inquiries, interpretation of clues, and use of scientific resources – supplemented by hunches, theories, and sometimes prejudices.

A much under-rated author of police procedurals is Janwillem van de Wetering. His portrait of Amsterdam is more realistic than Nicholas Freeling's, his detectives Grijpstra and de Gier far more human than Inspector Van der Valk. Some of his novels (like *The Corpse on the Dike*, 1976) contain real suspense, an unexpected solution, and evince a general attitude toward life, society, crime, criminals, and the law that is much closer to today's common scepticism than to the colour-blind defenders of law and order.

Sjöwall and Wahö are the most critically minded authors of 'police-procedural' novels; they are critical of bourgeois society as well as of the police. In *The Laughing Policeman*, the bourgeoisie's control of the media, used to suppress unpleasant truths, is impressively exposed.

Chester Himes's Harlem detectives (*A Rage in Harlem*, 1957; *Cotton Comes to Harlem*, 1968) are a case apart. These violent characters operate mainly against blacks, upholding white law. They do their duty because they are convinced that the black swindlers, gangsters, and murderers they are after make life even more miserable for Harlem inhabitants. But they hate it, God, how they hate it! Himes draws a convincing picture of the sometimes hilarious, sometimes grotesque Harlem scene, whose tragic background – injustice, humiliation and suffering – is ever present. His books sometimes seem to be realistic, even naturalistic novels masquerading as crime stories. One may acknowledge that basic realism without forgetting the regrettable reformism that clearly offers no fundamental way out for the majority of the oppressed blacks.

Chester Himes, incidentally, is living proof of a person's capacity to understand a milieu without ever having lived in it. In fact, he has never set foot in Harlem. As a black youth from Missouri, he spent seven and a half years in prison for criminal assault. This horrifying experience, and the traumatic self-consciousness of day-to-day encounter with anti-black racism in the US, determines all of his writings. These are by no means restricted to crime stories. (See, for example, his autobiographies *The Quality of Hurt*, 1972, and *My Life of Absurdity*, 1976.) Steven F. Milliken has written an interesting book about him.

In our view, by far the best police procedural is *La Nuit du Grand Boss* (1979), by the Italians Fruttero and Lucentini. (Previously, both authors had written a powerful satire of the Turin upper class in *La Donna della Domenica*, 1972.) Here nearly all the conventions of the genre have been abandoned. There is no individual hero. Commissario Santamaria is no more than the co-ordinator of a team in which an obscure feminist secretary accidentally discovers the key clue that exposes two murderers. It is also the sharpest denunciation of bourgeois society, far more effective than anything by Simenon, Dürrenmatt, or Sjöwall and Wahö. Fruttero and Lucentini use no eccentric billionaire who corrupts the authorities, and no lunatic tycoon bent on achieving world domination. They expose the real power of the head of a multinational (Fiat in this case) who dominates the city of Turin through an impenetrable network in which a section of the authorities, the church, Christian Democracy, the local Mafia, and the local football team play their part. It is not so much that the Boss strives to dominate his surroundings, but rather that he no longer even notices them. The portrait is far more credible – and more effective in its denunciation of the status quo – than the horror stories about the very rich that are found in so many thrillers today.

Fruttero and Lucentini have two additional qualities worthy of mention. Their approach to criminal investigations is never straightforward, but is ambiguous and many-sided. The story leaps from point to point like a movie camera, the angle of vision constantly altered. But it is woven together so skilfully that suspense is actually increased, and the reader never grows weary with the effort required to follow the intricacies of the plot.

Moreover, the style, and especially the dialogue, is brilliant. Even Hammett, Chandler, Ross Macdonald, and Hemingway seem somehow wooden in comparison. The realistic dialogue portrays the basic alienation of bourgeois society, as people desperately try to break out of isolation by communicating, and consistently fail to do so, speaking in syncopated and staccato sentences like these:

> 'Mama, please, we've found something that'…
> 'No, sorry, you listen. You get yourself hauled into the police station like a thief or God knows what all, sit around practically under arrest all afternoon, while I stand around crying on Mr Salle's shoulder, so his Saturday afternoon is ruined too, and he'…
> 'Mama, when I phoned, you weren't there.'
> 'I was on the way. As soon as Piera told me you'd been arrested again, I called a taxi and ran to'…
> 'Mama, I was not arrested. Look, here I am. And Graziano'…
> 'Then what are you doing here? Don't tell me it's coincidence.'

'It is. I already told the commissioner that Graziano'...
'Oh,' said Mrs Guidi, 'he's the one who found my lost little
girl. Then he must have known, and he wanted to surprise
me!'
'No, he didn't know anything, and when he found me sitting
in the stairwell'...
'Where is he now? I don't get it, what stairwell?'
'He went upstairs too, with Graziano.'
'Forget this Graziano. He was with you?'
'No, he was already up there. I waited for him a while in the
car, and then I went in too, and sat in the stairwell.'
'I don't get it, forget this stuff about a stairwell. Just tell me
why, while I'm running all over Turin like an idiot looking
for you, you hand me this wonderful surprise of'...
.(pp.174-75)

And even better:

'They all started talking at once.
"Extraordinary. It's a real"... (Picco). "Absolum. fant." (P.
Bono). "After *L'Elixir*, the best little book I ever... (the
famous D. P.). "Better than *L'Elixir*" (P. Bono). "You
should join the DIGOS, Professor"... (Cuoco, Fiora). "No?
That would be wonderful if you were with"... (P. Bono).
"Seriously, Professor, if you decided"... (Picco). "Maybe
you could help us with the *topos*"... (S. Maria). "Sure! I'm
sure that"... (P. Bono). "But Professor Gabarino"... (Picco).
"Congratulations, Professor. If we"... (Fiora, Guadagni,
Rappa). "No?"... (P. Bono). "But Professor Gabarino? Have
you already told him about your exceptional" (Picco). "What
the hell have I got to do with" (Monguzzi).' (pp.247-48)

7. From organized crime to state crime

With world war one and the period between the world wars, the general public became aware of a new sort of 'crime', one directed not against individual lives and property, but against the state. The perpetrators were not individuals acting for their own gain, but 'agents' of other governments and states. This widening interest in crimes of state – espionage above all – spawned an offspring of the detective story: the spy story. Once again, the history of crime is a key to the history of crime novels.

Espionage, of course, antedates the first world war, and the literary antecedants of the spy novel reach back into the nineteenth century. But the relatively new literary genre came of age quite rapidly after 1914, crossing the border between 'vulgar' and 'trivial' literature on the one hand and 'real' literature on the other. One reason is that many distinguished representatives of the intelligentsia were recruited by the British and American secret services during both world wars. Somerset Maugham is a case in point, as are, later, Graham Greene and quite a few others.

Julian Symons traces the origin of the spy novel back to James Fenimore Cooper's *The Spy* (1821) in which, significantly, the spy and not his opponent is the real hero. (The parallel with the 'good bandit' is obvious.) Symons then mentions William Le Queux, himself a former intelligence agent (*England's Peril*, 1899; *The Invasion of 1910*, 1910); Erskine Childers (*The Riddle of the Sands*, 1903); Joseph Conrad (*The Secret Agent*, 1907), whose literary qualities, however, place him in a different category; John Buchan (*The Thirty-Nine Steps*, 1915); and 'Sapper' (*Bulldog Drummond*, 1920).

The spy story attains maturity with Somerset Maugham's

Ashenden stories (1928) and Eric Ambler's pre-war novels (like *The Mask of Dimitrios*, 1938). But it was especially after world war two that the genre blossomed, with authors like John Le Carré (*The Spy Who Came in from the Cold*, 1963), Len Deighton (*The Ipcress File*, 1963), the more weakly constructed novels of the French writers Jean Bruce (*OSS 117 N'est Pas Mort*, 1953) and Dominique (*Le Gorille Vous Salue Bien*, 1955), and the German Johannes Mario Simmel, whose stories are spiced with much humour (*Es muss nicht immer Kaviar sein*, 1960). Graham Greene, a case apart, will be dealt with later.

A detailed history of the spy story could well begin with a chronicle of the vicissitudes of US foreign policy through the years of Cold War and detente, with the consequent shifts in the identities of the main villains: from Russians, to Chinese, to Cubans, to terrorists, to Arab oil sheikhs, to faceless, power-mad billionaires with private armies on small islands (like Gabriel in one of the Modesty Blaise novels), and then back to the Russians, now more often than not backing international terrorists. The plot of the spy novel is generally based on a conspiracy of the Enemy which is thwarted – usually at the very last minute – by Our Side's successful countermove against the Enemy in the Enemy's own camp. Although the odds are overwhelmingly against him, the Master Spy ultimately wins out, through a combination of greater physical fitness, superior technological prowess, better organization and sharper wits.

The parallel with the Super-brain of the classical detective story is evident. There is, of course, a solid dose of juvenile fantasizing in the James Bond style of super-spy, with physical, sexual, and technological exploits, but so was there in the classical heroes: Sherlock Holmes, Rouletabille, Arsène Lupin. But the heroes of Somerset Maugham, Graham Greene, and Eric Ambler are conspicuously lacking in such characteristics. Super-heroes must be raised to a higher level with the general development of bourgeois society: mounting mechanization, further growth of technology and the productive forces, greater diversification of commodity production, birth of the consumer society, further alienation of the individual, and the new and unforeseen dimensions of that alienation. Clearly, a super-spy cannot prevail armed solely with an analytical super-brain. And, during the Third Technological Revolution, is not expected to do so either.

In the spy story, unlike the usual detective story, the villains are normally well known from the outset, although occasionally their identification is one of the elements of the plot. They are agents of the Main Enemy of the State. The problem is not to identify them, but to undo their machinations. Nevertheless, the element of mystery is still very much with us. The allies, backers, means of operation, tactics, and often even purpose of the antagonist remain hidden. The Enemy's conspiracy cannot be defeated unless these are uncovered. The spy novel is therefore more similar to the detective story than it may appear at first sight.

But state crime is by no means limited to espionage. Just as espionage spills over into more general political intrigue, so the spy story pure and simple spawns the political thriller. Plots to kidnap or rescue opposition politicians under dictatorships (in so-called socialist countries as well as Western dictatorships), conspiracies to organize military coups in countries of Latin America and Africa, and also in Greece, Italy, and even the United States, attempts to capture, manipulate, or control the American president have all been the subjects of political thrillers. Eric Ambler, Graham Greene, Victor Canning and Morris West have all tried their hand at this genre. (In my view, West's novels *Harlequin* and *Salamander* qualify as 'real' literature, as of course does Uwe Johnson's *Mutmassungen über Jakob*, about a political murder in East Germany, and Robert Merle's *The Day of the Dolphin*.)

In real life, political intrigue and espionage can be woven together so intricately as to obscure or completely eliminate the boundary between 'legitimate' politics and criminal activity. The most striking case of the massive introduction of criminals into state affairs (first practised extensively by the Nazis) was the use of the Mafia by US military authorities during the second world war.

Perhaps the most radical manifestation of the all-pervasive moral ambiguity of the spy story is found in one of the most successful thrillers of recent years, Cruz Smith's *Gorky Park* (1981). This novel, set in Moscow, offers a compelling and convincing portrait of the motives, ideology, life style, and ubiquitous corruption of the middle layers of the Soviet bureaucracy.

But the hero, indeed the only honest person in the entire book, is a chief investigator of the Moscow Militia (in other words, the Soviet municipal police). The prime baddies are a New Yorker who is in business and is a murderer attempting to shatter a decade-old Russian monopoly in the world market for sable, and a Soviet state prosecutor who enters into a conspiracy with the American for reasons of greed. The American is an informer for both the KGB and the FBI, institutions which collaborate with one another sporadically. The KGB is presented as universally feared and hated in the USSR, but its leadership does act in the interests of the state. The FBI, on the other hand, seems motivated primarily by its corporate, parochial interests as an apparatus, covering up for murderers just as the KGB does, although for different purposes. What has become of the inalienable Right to Life, Liberty, and the Pursuit of Happiness? Extinguished, alas, by the ruthless competition between states, cast in the image of the ruthless competition between individual manufacturers of commodities and giant corporations.[1]

It should be noted that once again the transformation of content brings about a transformation of form and then adapts itself to it. Just as writers like Graham Greene and John Le Carré created the serious spy story, the *nouveau roman* appeared on the scene, opening a new chapter in the history of the novel. Among the leading practitioners of this new form are such outstanding novelists as the Russian Vladimir Nabokov, the Argentinian Borges, and the French Alain Robbe-Grillet. All three have written crime stories, albeit unusual ones: *Despair* (Nabokov), *Le Jardin aux Sentiers qui Bifurquent* (Borges), and *La Maison du Rendez-Vous* (Robbe-Grillet).

What is striking about these works is that they transcend, or even reverse, the classical 'reading' of clues. Traditionally, that reading is univocal: only one solution to the mystery is possible. In the novels of Nabokov, Borges, and Robbe-Grillet, on the contrary, there are several plausible readings of the clues, and the solution of the mystery remains multifarious and ambiguous. Indeed, *the* solution does not exist. This has led some literary critics to argue that the *nouveau roman* has fulfilled the potential implicit in the detective story but never realized. The *nouveau roman* is the *roman policier* finally become 'serious'.

The moral ambiguity of the spy story breeds cynicism. But there are many different kinds of cynics.

There are the mystifying cynics, like Ian Fleming (not to mention William Buckley or Gordon Liddy), who would have us believe that in the final analysis the world is still the arena of a struggle between Good and Evil. When confronting the 'faceless fur hats' of the Kremlin, or merciless organizations like SPEC-TRE, Good is inevitably compelled sometimes to resort to evil means.

Then there are the cynical cynics, who treat spies and counter-spies on the same footing. Their number is ever on the rise: Trevanian, Cruz Smith and many others.

Finally, there are the lucid cynics, who know that bourgeois society and commodity production are responsible, but believe that nothing can be done about it. Look at what is said about money as the root of all evil.

'Money is important in fiction because it is at the source of the most important fictions of our lives,' wrote David S. Gross in *Money Talks*. Reviewing the book in *The New York Times* (13 June 1981), Anatole Broyard aptly commented on these 'fictions' as viewed by successful authors: 'It is pleasant to reflect that most of the contemporary writers discussed in *Money Talks* have been paid a substantial amount of money for their fictions. It used to be thought that novelists wrote about money because they did not have it. Now they talk about it with all the eloquence of personal acquaintance.'

Better still, listen to William Goldman, who has an insane CIA-controlled doctor proclaim this liberal-democratic credo:

And don't tell me she was one of the God's good creatures, generous and kind to small animals — because humanism was always a dubious concept, one which fortunately is dying day by day. And don't tell me she was a painter, because until recent centuries artists were treated as little more than lepers, a position I don't find all that flawed. What matters today, all that matters today, is survival. And survival means weapon-ry. Superior weaponry. Period. End. (*Control*, 1982, p.262)

What spy thrillers and classical detective stories do have in common is the triple search for identity: who has done it; under what assumed identity is the villain hiding; what is the murderer – or spy, or mad billionaire, or conspirator – like as a 'person' (not as a human being, for the psychology of the crime story is generally too one-dimensional to allow complex and contradictory human beings to emerge).

Behind that search for identity lies one of the basic features of bourgeois society. The individual in that society is divided. As extractor of surplus value in the factory, as seller and buyer on the market, as capitalist competitor, the bourgeois or upper middle class person must be ruthless, immoral, full of guile and treachery, behaving like a 'criminal' even while respecting the 'rules of the game'.[2] But as citizens, individuals must respect equality: one person one vote, equal justice for everyone. As owners of private property they must ensure that their children will inherit their capital: hence the sanctity of marriage. But as men or women possessed of natural drives, of which the sexual drive is a fundamental one, they must look for satisfaction outside the family. Life is based on double standards, and consciousness is cleft from the beginning. Hence the individual drama, based on the contradiction between social norms and personal needs. Under normal conditions, this contradiction is restrained and repressed, especially when personal needs are frustrated. Crime and spy stories release these inhibitions, frustrations, and repressions, and allow the contradictions to flower. Behind the question 'whodunit?' there lurks, half hidden, the basic question of class society: 'Who are you really? Are you good or bad? Moral or immoral? God's creature or the devil's?' Except that you never *know* what you are, that the mass of humanity acts consciously in this society but without consciousness (or self-consciousness). In serious literature, this is reflected and reflected upon; women and men are both good and bad. In the detective story and the spy thriller, while this is increasingly understood too, the technique of the story itself implies a basic Manichaeanism of Good and Bad, all intentions to the contrary notwithstanding.

8. Mass production and mass consumption

The real massification of the detective story occurred with the paperback revolution, triggered off by the introduction of Penguin Books' first low-cost series and, in the United States, by the appearance of Simon and Schuster's Pocketbooks (with their adaptation of mass-marketing techniques to publishing), and by the need during world war two to print large numbers of cheap books for the US armed forces. In Germany, France and Britain, the practice of producing serious books in cheap, and often paperback, editions aimed at a wider market went back to before world war one, and formed part of the general expansion of publishing in this century. But given the dimensions of the American market and of the US military establishment during world war two, it was the mass production of paperbacks and pocketbooks for these that qualitatively altered the scope of both publishing and reading. Virtually overnight, thousands of readers became millions. Over the past twenty years, the total annual output of paperback books in English has regularly exceeded 1,000 million copies. And while cheap book production was by no means limited to so-called 'popular' literature – serious novels, classics, even scientific works and other non-fiction from the start shared the big press-runs – there can be no doubt that mystery stories accounted for a very substantial proportion of this expanded output.

Although it is impossible to give an exact figure, between a quarter and a third of total paperback output could probably be put into the category of 'thrillers' of one kind or another. It is no exaggeration to say that, since 1945, at least 10,000 million copies of crime stories have been sold world-wide. English has been easily the top language, followed at a considerable distance by French, Spanish, German and Japanese: annual French sales top 30 million, annual German sales are put at 20-25 million, annual Japanese sales moved from some 14 million in the mid sixties to 20 million in the mid seventies. Best-selling authors to date have been Agatha Christie, with world sales of 500 million copies, Edgar Wallace with 300 million, Georges Simenon with 300 million, the German Jerry Cotton series with 300 million, Mickey Spillane with 150 million, Alistair MacLean with 150 million, Ian Fleming's James Bond series with 100 million, Frederic Forsyth with 100 million, San Antonio with 100 million.

The paperback revolution came as a godsend to the crime story at the very moment the genre was suffering from a stagnating, if not declining, market. Most crime story authors only sold a few thousand copies at the most in the 1930s, read by the same lending-library addicts. (Philip van Doren Stern in Howard Haycraft, op.cit. p.531) Only the paperback revolution created a market extending to millions of new readers.

The question is: why? What explains the extraordinary attraction of the crime novel? What basic psychological need, in tens of millions of people, did and does the detective story satisfy? Why did that need become particularly acute at a specific point in time – roughly speaking from the 1930s to the 1950s – rather than fifty years earlier, say, or thirty years later? We know that a commodity can have no exchange-value if it does not have a use-value. The colossal commercial success of the detective story bears witness to the existence of such a use-value. But what exactly is it?

When we speak of a psychological need, we must take care to define the term more precisely if we are to avoid ahistorical – and therefore incorrect – assumptions. For it is not uncommon to encounter simplistic references to some unconscious aggressive drive, instinctive blood lust, or death wish, that is seen as underpinning the detective story's popularity. Now it seems self-evident that such unconscious drives, impulses, unavowed passions and repressed appetites, the legacy of our species's brute or animal past, make the popularity and mass consumption of crime stories *possible*. But what is possible is by no means always realized. The difficulty with explaining the rise of mass-produced detective stories in the terms of human passions and impulses is the same as with all attempts to account, by individual psychology, for phenomena that are basically historical: it is unconvincing to explain changes by factors permanently at work; in other words, to explain change by absence of change, movement by stability, discontinuity by continuously operating forces.

After all, aggressive drives, blood lust and the death wish were certainly present two thousand, five hundred, or two hundred years ago. In most geographico-cultural areas, innumerable expressions of them are to be found throughout social life – in warfare or other forms of violence, in religions and cults, in artistic and literary creation – but they have not been expressed in the mass production and consumption of crime stories. So to limit one's explanation of the massive explosion of this specific literary genre mainly or solely to such factors of individual psychology is really to explain nothing of what is specific about the mystery story. Obviously, these factors of individual psychology have to be integrated, or subsumed, into the more general phenomenon of *social evolution*. The real question then becomes clear: what social environment, what social pressures, made men and women (consciously or unconsciously, in proportions that remain to be determined) satisfy certain impulses – including, if you wish, aggressive drives, blood lust and death wish – by buying and reading crime novels?

Let us begin by stating the obvious, since however obvious it may be, it has somehow been missed by many commentators on the crime story's popular success. Reading about violence is an (innocent) form of witnessing, and enjoying, violence – albeit perhaps in a shuddering, shameful and guilt-ridden way. It implies the simultaneous maturation of two phenomena: on the one hand, mass literacy, with the spread of universal schooling up to the age of 14 or 15; on the other hand, the abandonment of actually practised violence in favour of vicariously experienced violence (in the Wild West, insofar as it really existed, cowboys did not have to read about shooting it out; they practised it themselves).

In this sense, the mass consumption of crime stories is a phenomenon of growing civilization. It is better to read about murders than to commit murder oneself. Moreover, the temporal framework within which this particular form of sublimation becomes possible at once enables one to locate, with some degree of accuracy, the moment at which the detective story becomes massified. Given the historical dynamics of mass literacy – and the economic needs that induced it – it could not have occurred much earlier than it actually did. Even a phenomenon as simple as a reference language (vocabulary) commonly understood by millions is of quite recent origin: through most of the nineteenth century, the 'lower' and 'upper' classes had quite distinct vocabularies.

But if the mass consumption of detective stories is proof of a certain degree (let us even admit, progress) of civilization, it also expresses the partial, contradictory, and self-negating nature of that civilization. After all, there are higher, nobler and more humane ways of sublimating aggressive drives than by reading about murders. Bourgeois civilization is simultaneously civiliza- tion and rebellion against civilization; civilization and non- (or half-) assimilated civilization. It is civilization imposed by the hidden hand of market laws, by the iron rules of factory discipline, and by the despotism of the nuclear family, authoritarian schools, and repressive sexual education (or lack of education), all tending to impose a tyrannical discipline upon individuals from above.

It is civilization imposed by laws that are respected not out of conviction but out of fear of punishment. It is civilization born of – and leading to – countless frustrations. The production of ever new commodities, for which ever new appetites must be aroused, is one of the mechanisms that make the ever enlarged reproduction of capital possible. And it is civilization born of violence and leading to ever enlarged violence at the margins of 'civilized life': violence against colonial peoples; violence against the poor; violence against foreigners; violence against the non-conforming; violence against women; occasionally, violence against the proletariat itself when in revolt. Is it strange, under these circumstances, that the sublimation of violent drives should take the frustrated form of harking back to vicarious violence?

To understand the mass expansion of the crime story that began in the thirties and forties, we must relate it to another social phenomenon too: the transformation of the 'old' into the 'new' middle classes. As the number of independent farmers, artisans and tradespeople declined, the number of technicians, clerical workers and employees in the so-called service industries rose. Wage-labour was introduced on a massive scale into the so-called professions. These social transformations implied a huge extension of the capitalist organization of labour, to which millions of people were newly subjected. It was among these people (and only incidentally in the higher layers of the industrial proletariat) that the mass market for detective novels was to be found. (According to Colin Watson (*Crime Writers*), Agatha Christie's readers are 'respectable' suburban people, especially women: the private lending libraries were a fortress of Christie-devotees. Alistair MacLean's readers, according to John Sutherland (*Fiction and the Fiction Industry*, p. 97), are mainly men, low- to middle-brow, middle-class or slightly above, and middle-aged or above. According to a poll organized for Dilys Winn's *Murder Ink* (p. 440) – unless this is a hoax – the readers of mystery novels are mostly between 25 and 35, claim to have college degrees, and are most frequently (in decreasing order) lawyers, copywriters, school-teachers, librarians and women who work at home — at least in the United States. The need for the type of reading provided by the crime story can, therefore, be traced back to specific collective psychological requirements of these social layers, under the impact of their objective proletarianization.

The decline of farming and huge exodus from the countryside, the monstrous growth of metropolitan conurbations (much faster in the mid twentieth than in the mid nineteenth century), the lengthening distance between home and work, the increasing pollution of the atmosphere by dirt and noise, the intensification of nervous strain exemplified by the conveyer belt: all these phenomena create a powerful need for *distraction*. This need is satisfied by cigarettes and alcohol, by the movies, and also, among literate layers of the population, by the crime story – as, at a later stage, it will increasingly be by television, much of which will have an analogous function and content.

The detective story becomes the opium of the 'new' middle classes in the real sense of Marx's original formula: as a psychological drug that distracts from the intolerable drudgery of daily life.[1] While you read it, your attention is captured to such an extent that you forget everything else — and heaven knows it is worth forgetting! Yet, as Leo Kofler notes, it is an opium of a special kind: whereas religion purports to offer human self-realization in a fantastic form, drugs attempt to realize human freedom in a purely destructive way (*Soziologie des Ideologischen*, p. 118). One should only add that crime stories attempt to realize distraction in a purely passive way, without any effort or sacrifice by the middle-class individual. They not only capture ('suspend') the attention, they also titillate the nerves in a particular, deliciously naughty way.

We can now extend what Marx said about the criminal breaking the monotony and everyday security of bourgeois life to a much broader public. The increasing proletarianization of intellectual and 'service' labour, and the growth of the 'new' middle classes, do not mean only increased nervous tension for millions of people. They also mean increased monotony, uniformity, and standardization of work and life. But this in turn produces a need for some at least temporary escape. For a literate population, the crime story becomes an ideal means to escape from the monotony of daily life into vicariously enjoyed adventures. The craved security of a sheltered existence, the material ideal of the middle classes, is counterbalanced by a vicarious insecurity. Readers carry out in fantasy what they secretly long to do but never will in real life: to upset the applecart.

An interesting and parallel explanation has been advanced by a distinguished New York psychoanalyst, Dr Edmund Bergler:

> What these facts do prove is the enormous amount of inner passivity in people. Since, in seeing or reading a thriller, this inner passivity can be enjoyed with two face-saving alibis ('I am aggressive' and 'The whole thing is only a game'), the attraction is irresistible to some, especially since it is coupled with enjoyment of childlike megalomania resuscitated by the appearance of the uncanny. These millions of mystery fans do not represent the reservoir of 'potential murderers' but are, criminologically speaking, harmless. These people get temporary release of their tensions vicariously.

Finally, there is nothing so astonishing about the fact that literate people should be obsessed with mystery stories. After all, as Ernst Bloch once pointed out: isn't the whole of bourgeois society operating like a big mystery, anyway? Here you are, toiling away assiduously at your small business, and all of a sudden this business collapses, for mysterious reasons (prices start to fall, rates of interest rise, markets shrink), through no fault of your own. Here you are, slaving away at your job, obeying all the rules imposed by machines and foremen, pushing yourself as hard as you can in the rat race, and then you are still fired. Worse, you are unexpectedly hit by a recession, a long depression, even a war. Who is responsible for all this? You aren't. Nor are your neighbours or acquaintants. Some mysterious behind-the-scene conspirators must have something to do with it. Let at least some of the mysteries be cleared up, and you'll feel less alienated.

Bertolt Brecht made a similar point:

> We gain our knowledge of life in a catastrophic form. It is from catastrophes that we have to deduce the manner in which our social community functions. By reflection, we must decide the 'inside story' of crises, depressions, revolutions, and wars. We sense even from reading the newspapers (but also bills, letters of dismissal, call-up papers and so forth) that somebody must have done something for the open catastrophe to have arisen. What then has this person done? Behind the events that we are told about, we suspect other occurrences about which we are not told. These are the real occurrences. Only if we knew would we understand. Only history can inform us about these real occurrences – insofar as the actors have not succeeded in keeping them entirely secret. History is written *after* catastrophes. This basic situation, in which intellectuals feel that they are objects and not subjects of history, moulds the thought which they can display for enjoyment in the crime story. Existence depends upon unknown factors. 'Something must have happened', 'something is brewing', 'a situation has arisen' – this is what they feel, and the mind goes out on patrol. But enlightenment only comes, if at all, after the

catastrophe. The death has taken place. What had been brewing beforehand? What had happened? Why has a situation arisen? All this can now perhaps be deduced.

The crime story is a response to the needs of alienated intellectual and service-industry labour, partially conscious of its alienation but not yet sufficiently so to understand that a scientific explanation of the mysteries of commodity production and bourgeois society is possible, and that collective emancipation is preferable to individual escapism. It is semi-emancipatory, as it is semi-civilized and semi-sublimating. It is bourgeois *par excellence*, bourgeois medicine for the middle class sufferers from the ills of bourgeois society.

Moreover, it is as reified as it is bourgeois, since the *social causes* of human problems are presented as *things*, quite literally. For instance, in *The Green Ripper* (1979), one of a long series of reactionary novels by John D. MacDonald, the author's egghead representative Meyer explains the rising threat of barbarism in the following way:

The real world is out there in a slow, dreadful process of change. There is a final agony of millions out there, and one and a quarter million new souls arriving every week. We try to think about it less than we used to. None of it makes any sense, really. But then whatever *it* is out there, *it* moves into this world in the shape of a tiny sphere of platinum and iridium and deadly poison. Now we have to think about it, but *it cannot be personalized*. It is all a *thing, a great plated toad-lizard thing* with rotten breath, squatting back inside the mouth of the cave, infinitely patient. (pp. 112-13, emphasis added)

Two recent successful thrillers illustrate the obsession of authors, readers, and the whole intellectual climate, with conspiracies as a substitute for any scientific attempt to explain the mysteries – in other words, the laws of motion – of society. In *The Parsifal Mosaic* (1982), Robert Ludlum weaves a fairly implausible tale of reciprocal infiltration by the US and Soviet governments, until nobody knows any longer who is manipulating whom. Thousands of miles away, the Russian emigre writer Vladimir Volkhov published a similar story in French, *Le Montage*. His obsession with infiltration is such that a large part of the Russian dissident community in exile is presented as being itself manipulated by the KGB! Only a profoundly sick society can see the world as dominated by manipulation, with hardly anyone able to determine or control their own convictions, let alone actions, and with everybody becoming the puppets of mysterious 'agencies'. Yet is this not, in fact, just how alienated humankind sees its social fate in bourgeois society?

9. Outward diversification

Mass production requires a mass market. It can create a mass market for goods not previously available, provided that a latent, potential need exists. As I have already indicated, mass-produced crime stories do indeed satisfy a latent need of this kind, among broad masses of potential readers from the lower middle classes and the more literate layers of white collar workers.

But the mass production of crime stories involves two stages, writing and publishing. The publishing stage is essentially a mechanical one. A relatively small revolution in printing technology made the mass production of paperback books possible. The real technological revolution in the printing industry came almost twenty years later, with the arrival of photocomposition. And the real technological challenge to mass-produced paperbacks is coming with the video cassette.

The broadening of the market, however, also leads inevitably to a broader range of authors, with diversification of tastes, sensibilities and needs. It would be impossible for millions of readers all to enjoy exactly the same idiosyncrasies of the same detectives; to be satisfied with stories set in the same milieu; or with mysteries constructed on the same pattern. Not everyone can appreciate Lord Peter Wimsey's humour, Charlie Chan's apologetic sing-song, or Ellery Queen's eccentricities – though hundreds of thousands of readers did, and, decreasingly, still do. Not everyone can see the world as centred on the drawing-room of the English country house.

So the explosion of the market meant an inevitable explosion in the number of authors catering for a new diversity of tastes. Anybody with any experience in the field of crime detection might be tempted to try their hand at crime writing, for the rewards were high indeed. As the line between popular penny-sheets and 'real' detective stories became thinner and thinner, more and more authors sought to cross it. The trajectory of the great Dashiell Hammett is illustrative here: from being a Pinkerton agent, he became a pulp-magazine writer before blossoming into a classical detective-story author.

A more detailed history of the detective story, especially in the thirties and forties, would also involve a history of pulp magazines in the twenties and even prior to the first world war. Interesting parallels would appear, opening up a whole new perspective upon the origin and dynamics of certain classic forms of the modern crime novel. The pulp magazines, written for children and the semi-literate, often reworked themes taken from the 'high' literature of two or three generations before. Fenimore Cooper and Hiawatha were inspiration for the innumerable Buffalo Bill stories (in Germany, courtesy of Karl May).[1] There is, of course, an exact parallel between the cowboy/Indian dichotomy and that of detective and criminal. So the superhuman exploits of Sherlock Holmes in his struggle against crime and evil were replicated thirty years later in countless pulp series, like the one that starred Nick Carter.

The attempt by American bourgeois society to rationalize and justify its original sin – the genocide of the continent's indigenous population – laid an ideological foundation for that society's self-justification for its current sins: its systematic defence of private property, regardless of the cost in human misery or the consequences for the fate of humanity, and its labelling as criminals of all violators of that property. Millions who, as children, had been trained to see things in red-or-white terms by the 'Injun' pulp magazines would, as grown-ups, readily accept the black-or-white polarities of the crime story. It took the full impact upon American society of the colonial revolution (especially as viewed through the prisms of the Vietnam War and the civil-rights movement in the sixties) before the cowboy/Indian relationship – with its cops-and-robbers reflection in the mass-market detective story – was fundamentally reversed for millions, with the Indians becoming the true heroes. (This was in fact more successfully expressed in the cinema, with movies like *Soldier Blue* and *Cheyenne*, but literature made its contribution too.)

As crime writers multiplied, some of the more successful carried out new variations of their detective-heroes. Agatha Christie created Miss Marple alongside Hercule Poirot; J. Dickson Carr had Sir Henry Merrivale take the place of Gideon Fell; Erle Stanley Gardner substituted Donald Lam for Perry Mason, and, later, Quiller's Adam Hall was, happily, to replace his Hugo Bishop.

But the limits are evident. If millions of readers wanted to consume detective stories, the need for more detectives meant a proliferation of authors. In their hands, the original super-hero spread out like a Chinese fan. In addition to every kind of police under the sun, those who chased murderers now came to include pure geniuses (sitting in their armchairs while the actual chasing was done by nimble acolytes), nobility, men-about-town, yacht-racers, bankers, country ladies, motorboat experts, retired financial wizards, psychiatrists, priests, rabbis, teachers, university lecturers, army officers (active and retired), *mafiosi* (active and retired), doctors, jockeys, civil servants, diplomats, scientists from all manner of specialist fields, journalists, actors, television people, industrialists, spies and spy-chasers of every description, and plain insufferable busybodies. The only type of detective we have not yet encountered are normal industrial workers or farmers. But even this may be temporary.[2]

The settings of the detectives' exploits also grew more diverse. Like the seat of real world power, the scene of the detective novel moved away from the English country house, the London club, or the Paris mansion. Occasionally it may revisit them with transient nostalgia, but the general movement is decisively away from the old centres to all points of the compass: to New York, Washington DC, California, Florida and Hawaii; to the Côte d'Azur, the French provinces, Brussels, Liège, Amsterdam, Stockholm and Helsinki; to Berlin, Hamburg, Munich, Frankfurt and Bonn; to Rome, Venice, Florence and the Tuscan countryside, with a bit of Sicily thrown in for good measure; to Spain, Portugal, Greece, the Topkapi Museum in Istanbul, and the Levant; to Australia and New Zealand, Brazil, the Caribbean islands, Tanzania, Bombay, Hong Kong, Seoul, Singapore and Tokyo; even to Moscow and

Peking, not to mention the GDR, Warsaw, Prague, Budapest, and Montenegro. A whiff of exoticism and local colour will no longer do; what we are getting now is next year's holiday brochures, with all the works: an unending travelogue covering the whole globe – and soon to the moon?[3]

Evelyn Waugh once remarked that real travel books had gone out of fashion after world war two. The real meaning of this snobbish pronouncement was that international travel by the elite of imperial administrators, bankers, mining engineers, diplomats, and the idle rich (with the occasional soldier-of-fortune, art lover, university student, or international salesperson on the fringes) was being swamped by lower-middle-class mass tourism, so that books for travellers had to take this new broader market into account. The Fodor travel-guide has replaced the classical Baedeker. And mass-produced paperbacks could fulfil a useful ancillary function by giving millions of future (or former) tourists a foretaste (reminiscence) of lands to be discovered (once visited).

This particular feature of the modern crime story is merely one expression of a more general phenomenon. With the broadening of its market, the initial function of the genre had to be broadened. It was no longer enough to thrill readers, to lull them into forgetfulness, or to help them to live vicarious lives that standardized work and a standardized existence would never allow them to live in reality. The novel was increasingly obliged to provide additional services. The growth of the market itself furnished the stimulus for a secondary function of the detective story. A mass market implied hard competition, but since this was monopolistic competition with rigidly fixed prices, and since production costs were about the same – and irreducible – throughout the industry, price competition was excluded. The only way to get the edge over competitors was to endow one's commodities with additional use-value, to provide additional services.

The service the crime story could offer, aside from straight-forward 'entertainment', was to provide condensed, standardized, specialist knowledge in innumerable fields of human endeavour. From the late thirties and early forties (the heyday of a Rex Stout) to the seventies and early eighties (the period of an Adam Hall), the list has been growing. The reader has been given a crash course in forensic medicine and courtroom procedure (Erle Stanley Gardner); orchid-growing and *haute cuisine* (Rex Stout); the theatre and painting (Ngaio Marsh); the real-estate business and local capital accumulation in Florida, as well as motorboat lore (John D. MacDonald); horse-racing and photography (Dick Francis); the Talmud (Kemelman); Californian irrigation laws (Ross Macdonald); confidence trickery in Harlem (Chester Himes); nuclear-power plants (John Gardner); banking and its involvement with commercial sport, the antique trade, and much else (Emma Lather); hijacking techniques (Alistair MacLean); stockmarket operations, commodity options, and currency speculation (Paul Erdman); the oil business (countless authors); electronics (Sanders); the illegal marketing of parts of the human body (Robin Cook); the umbilical relationship of politicians with organized crime in the United States (innumerable authors following Dashiell Hammett); the installation of 'impregnable' security systems; the detection of miniaturized surveillance gadgets; rocketry; space technology; gambling (Ian Fleming and others); cheating at cards; make-up and disguise; the conditions of existence of Soviet generals and KGB chiefs; the standing orders of the Spanish Communist Party's Central Committee meetings – and so on *ad infinitum*.

Historical settings for crime stories become increasingly fashionable. After the Dutch writer van Gulik's Judge Dee series, set in seventh-century classical China, the German writer Heinz-Dieter Stövers (*Mord auf der Via Appia*, 1972) has given a late-Roman-Republic setting to a series of crime stories called *CVT im Dienste der Cäsaren*. Frederick Nolan locates his *No Place to Be a Cop* in New York in 1878. And there is Umberto Eco's *The Name of the Rose*, one of the most sophisticated crime stories ever written, laid in a fourteenth-century Italian monastery.

This packaged expert knowledge often represents months of research, sometimes by whole teams of researchers, as with a television programme. The authors, at least in the higher brackets of the craft, can hardly ever be faulted even on the most trivial detail. (Only very rarely does Homer nod: Elleston Trevor – Adam Hall – in *The Peking Target* called Admiral Carrero Branco Spain's president; he was prime minister, of course – but who really cares?). And even if John Sutherland (*Fiction and the Fiction Industry*) does find the presentation of Michael Crighton's *The Andromeda Strain* a hoax, mere mystificatory mumbo-jumbo, can the information on the plague contained in the book be so summarily dismissed?

Some of the expertise displayed by crime writers is of personal origin. Dick Francis was a jockey. Ngaio Marsh was involved in the theatre for years. Erle Stanley Gardner was indeed a lawyer. Somerset Maugham, Graham Greene, Ian Fleming, Pierre Nord and San Antonio were all once in the spy business (so too was Johannes Mario Simmel – or was he?). Dashiell Hammett and Raymond Chandler were trained in real private-detective agencies, the German author Ky was indeed a criminologist as is P.D. James; Robin Cook and Michael Crighton studied medicine, and Frances Lockridge did keep house. Umberto Eco is a medievalist and best of all, Roger Borniche (*Le Playboy*, 1976) – who is in real life a police officer – presents as his hero a police officer called Roger Borniche. So all these authors knew what they were writing about. In other cases, the expert knowledge has been gathered painstakingly, whether as general background for a whole series or book by book, as with Victor Canning's or Desmond Bagley's thrillers: the description of the build-up of an avalanche in Bagley's *Snow Tiger* (1975) might have come straight out of a scientific handbook.

This expertise is a relatively recent development though. Earlier writers, among them many classics, were notoriously deficient and evoked strong criticism on that account. Raymond Chandler's *The Simple Art of Murder* says much of the obvious about it, as do J. B. Waite's *The Lawyer Looks at Detective Fiction* (in Howard Haycraft's *The Art of the Mystery Story*) and Edmund Wilson's *Who Cares Who Killed Roger Ackroyd?* also in Haycraft (the article first appeared in 1945 in *The New Yorker*).[4]

At times the specialized knowledge thus dispensed becomes so copious that it starts to crowd out the plot and all suspense: the ancillary service displaces the book's primary function. If enough readers are prepared to accept this, then we have a new case of autonomization: division of labour following the implacable logic of commodity production and reification.

There is obviously more involved here than simple pleasure in an easy way of learning. Under late capitalism, we are living in the age of the third technological revolution. Interest in technology is being given a tremendous boost by schools, the mass media and advertising. At the same time, for the middle-aged and older generations in particular, modern technology (even in the more elementary form of household electronic devices) is seen as a mysterious and frightening universe that eludes human understanding and control. Fascination with space, and myths about UFOs and extra-terrestrial aliens are mingled with anxiety about the invasion of privacy and daily life by secret mechanical devices in the service of an ever more sophisticated and pervasive apparatus of state information and surveillance.

Thus the outward diversification of the crime story is closely linked to the third technological revolution and the new anxieties it has helped to spawn. As John Sutherland aptly puts it in relation to the medical thriller and especially Robin Cook's books (*Fiction and the Fiction Industry*, pp.213-14):

> At what might be taken as its surface level, *Coma* alludes to current anxieties about medical treatment which preoccupy the thinking American. In a preview, *Publishers Weekly* (7 February 1977) advertised it as containing 'horrifying revelations about present-day hospital scandals'. 'Indirect allusion to' rather than 'revelation of' is the correct formulation; but the present-day scandals or anxieties clearly in *Coma's* frame of reference are: 1. the prevalence of iatrogenic, or doctor-induced illness; 2. the ethics of transplant operations; 3. the 'legal definition of death' controversy …; 4. the malpractice suits and the vast damages increasingly awarded by American courts to patients who could prove faulty or incompetent treatment; 5. the crippling cost of medical treatment in the US, and the successful resistance to medicare by the AMA and interest lobbies. As a result, the first conscious thought of most postoperative American patients is, supposedly, not 'Am I cured?' but 'How am I going to pay for all this?'

Of course there is a lot here that is not really new. Fear of hospitals as terrifying places – which they have indeed been for poor people – was deeply ingrained in the reading public during the nineteenth century. Anxiety about the cost of medical treatment is as old as modern capitalist (paid) medicine, and by no means a product of recent technological or economic changes. Indeed, in many West European countries it has declined with the rise of the welfare state, and has been reappearing only as a result of the cuts in social expenditure that have followed in the wake of the present economic depression and austerity policies. At the same time, recent technological advances have clearly introduced a whole new dimension, and, more generally, the relationship seems quite clear between the 'information-packed' thriller and the anxieties about technology triggered off under late capitalism.

Nevertheless, the social function of the crime novel still remains what it has always been: to distract, revitalize, and thrill; to lift the reader out of the limbo of nervous strain induced by standardized and monotonous work and daily existence. So the average reader will rarely accept the substitution of 'pure' information for 'pure' thrills. The opposite is rather the case. In the background of the sophisticated and 'serious' crime story, there still hovers the vulgar, infantile, raw crime novel. Although nowadays perhaps only children and adolescents read the primeval models — Nick Carter, Edgar Wallace, Sax Rohmer, Mickey Spillane — their progeny, reproducing the bare essentials of the genre, are devoured by millions of literate adults. Here, all specialized knowledge is dispensed with, as is any intricate subtlety of plot. What is left is the cops-and-robbers theme reduced to its caricatural core. Often the ideological function of the whole thing will be revealed by some incidental aside, as when Bulldog Drummond's pathological hatred of everything and everybody not British and not bourgeois is faithfully reproduced, almost half a century later, in the outlook of George Shipway's *The Chilean Club* (1972), in which a quartet of veterans get together in St James's to liquidate the trade-union officials, student leaders and Trotskyist scum who are ruining 'their' Britain.

10. Inward diversification

Some critics have contended that, from the moment the detective story went into mass production, degeneration set in. The finely constructed mechanism stopped ticking. The actions and motives of suspects were no longer submitted to searching analysis; the suspects were simply beaten up. Routine police procedures or information from stool-pigeons now took the place of the superhuman intellect in solving a mystery.

There is an element of snobbery, however, in this misguided judgement. From the point of view of intellectual prowess or analytical deduction, Nero Wolfe is certainly not inferior to Sherlock Holmes. From the point of view of the general rules and inner logic of the craft, there is improvement rather than decline from Gaston Leroux to Georges Simenon, from Earl Biggers or Dorothy Sayers (though not from Anthony Berkeley) to Ross Macdonald or John Le Carré. And with all due respect to the 'queen of crime', Len Deighton and Adam Hall do write better English than Agatha Christie. It is true that Dashiell Hammett and Raymond Chandler have qualities hardly matched thereafter, as does Georges Simenon. But these qualities are related to a specific watershed in the crime story's development, its coming of age rather than the beginning of its decline. What ensued was maturity, not degeneration: another set of qualities, another standard of sophistication, not to be encountered among the classics and induced by stronger competition. Lord Peter Wimsey's adventures in crime-detecting continue to entertain, but it is hard to deny that, in sheer, nerve-tingling suspense, *Marathon Man, Coma,* or even *The Andromeda Strain*, are masterpieces that no classic of the twenties or thirties can equal.

Does this judgement raise a problem of definition? Should the category of 'detective story' be reserved for the whodunit pure and simple, with spy stories and thrillers treated as separate genres? We do not think so. The 'mystery' of a crime story may lie in any one or several of its basic elements, or in all of them: who, whom, where, when, why, by what means, how (the opportunity). There is no reason why it should refer only to the 'who'. (Indeed, even in the classic detective story this is not always the case, witness Anthony Berkeley's *Trial and Error*.) Once this is granted, the thriller – in which the 'who' is either known from the outset, or irrelevant, or secondary to some other purpose of the book – may be considered a legitimate offspring of the detective story, provided rules are respected.

Even so, questions remain. Why did the spy story and the thriller often closely related to it (Fleming, Le Carré, Deighton, Hall, some of Canning, most of Macdonald) diverge from the original whodunit? And why at a specific moment in time? What is the inner logic of this diversification? As we have already pointed out, the spy story is a product of the hypertrophy of the espionage establishment, the intelligence services of the great powers and their military apparatuses; hence a product of the growth of armies, of the arms race, and of war. It was initially a direct product of world war one, and underwent vast expansion on the eve of, during, and in the aftermath of world war two – an expansion that continued during the successive stages of the Cold War.

However, there is a more fundamental quality of the thriller and spy novel that justifies treating them as distinct sub-species of the original detective story, despite all that they have in common. The detective outwits the criminal essentially by means of logical prowess. The paraphernalia of the trade – Sherlock Holmes's magnifying glass or chemical retorts – are mere secondary tools, subordinated entirely to Reason. The criminal, too, is clever, and often outwits the police, but cannot outwit the great detective's super-brain.

Here we have the purest, most elementary expression of bourgeois society: commodity production and commodity circulation under conditions of perfect competition. Everything is rational, totally geared to the maximization of income (profits), through continual cuts in production costs and sales costs (including profit margins). All's well that ends well. In the end, rational individual economic behaviour by all will bring the maximum well-being (including the satisfaction of the consumer) to the maximum number of individuals. Let the best one win (Sherlock Holmes, not the criminal), and this will be good for everybody, including the criminal (if not for his body, at least for his immortal soul).

With the transition from competitive to monopoly capitalism, this mythical ideal world – which in any case never bore more than a limited resemblance to the real functioning of the economy – lost all relevance for explaining how society actually operates. For in reality, meritocracy is a mystification. The best person hardly ever wins. To come out on top in the rat race, it is not necessary to have the best brains, most energy, or even the strongest will-power or ego. What you need is the largest capital, running into billions. Once you have that, you can hire the best brains, assemble the drive and energy of dozens of top experts, create a collective will ('the organization') that can either harness the strongest egos or break them if they will not conform.

The thriller (including the spy thriller) is to the detective story what monopoly capitalism is to the capitalism of free competition. To enter its characteristic plots, armed only with one's wits (even those of the formidable Nero Wolfe) is like challenging a multinational corporation with only five thousand pounds sterling in one's bank account. Qualities like wit, energy, and will-power have become secondary, even negligible paraphernalia. The hero – whether super-spy, super-sleuth, super-adventurer, or super-rescuer (like Travis McGee) – will win only through a combination of greater technical resources (including, frequently, big money, to be acquired by special means), greater physical fitness, superior organization, and (usually in last place) quicker wits. The relative decline of pure intellect, pure *ratio*, in the detective story is a striking reflection of the relative decline of rationalism in bourgeois ideology, and of the rational (or allegedly rational) behaviour of *homo oeconomicus* under mature and late capitalism.

Chronology is not really a problem here. It is true that monopoly capitalism made its appearance in about 1885 or 1890, well before the turn of the century. But the mental structures that determine basic ideology generally lag behind objective reality by at least two generations – as does popular behind avant-garde literature. So we should expect the thriller and spy story to emerge as separate genres derived from the original detective novel, with a broad popular market, in the late thirties. And this is indeed what occurred. With *The Thirty-Nine Steps* as its first real precursor, the genre proper appeared on the scene in the thirties with John P. Marquand's *Mr Moto* series (in which, incidentally, the Japanese spy was still the hero and the Chinese the villains!)

Dominant mental structures are one thing; actually experienced motives, needs and frustrations are something quite different. It would not be hard to prove that conformism, conveyor-belt labour, mass-produced consumer goods, standardized leisure, big-city loneliness and alienation, small-town boredom and alienation, a daily life devoid of light, warmth, or even the hope of adventure, finally came to dominate the lower middle class, white collar workers, and the better-paid blue collar workers with the advent of late capitalism in the middle forties in the USA, the late forties and early fifties in Western Europe and Japan. Under these circumstances the thriller and spy novel gained their broad popular appeal, an appeal wider in fact than the original classic or post-classic 'pure' detective story had ever enjoyed. From this viewpoint, the tough, realistic detective novels of the Hammett/Chandler/Simenon/Ross Macdonald school were simply a transitional form between the drawing-room mystery and the world-wide adventure; Mike Hammer was a bridge between Holmes and Poirot on the one hand and Bond and Quiller on the other, just as Carnegie's US Steel Corporation or Krupp were a bridge between the free-enterprise industrial firms of the 1850s and the true multinational corporations of the 1950s.

The key to the inner transformation of the genre lies in the evolution from *thinking* to *acting*. The classic detectives do not act, they think. In an extreme case like that of Nero Wolfe, he does not even move, except from the ground floor of his Manhattan brownstone to the upper floors, by elevator. He is pure, distilled brain-power. Today, however, intellectual specialization of this kind, physical sloth and limitless gourmandise, are no longer the readers' fantasy, even in guilty dreams: they would be more likely to pity poor fatso these days than to envy him.

James Bond and his offspring are something else again. They are all action. Action now counts for much more than any power of reasoning. And the type of action is one the masses can readily identify with, involving as it does speed, travel to faraway places, sexual prowess, luxury living, danger, physical fitness, access to the latest gadgetry and secrets of state, the backstage manipulation of events. Infantile daydreams? Undoubtedly. Yet this is what millions of readers wish to identify with and vicariously enjoy, knowing that they will never live them.

Physical fitness has come to play an increasingly important role in all this, a fact which is obviously linked to the changed consumer priorities of the ruling class, slowly trickling down to the middle classes. In the third world, hunger is still dominant. For the lower ranks of the proletariat too, the fear of hunger is still very real: bad diet is still the wage-earner's fate whenever there is a sudden drop in income. But for several generations now the middle classes have been freed from all fears in this domain. They are no longer worried about not getting enough to eat, they are worried about overeating, and in general about their bodily health. The physical-fitness ideal implies a preoccupation with the human body that was entirely absent from nineteenth-century literature, and that breaks out in the most extreme form in thrillers in which scenes of unarmed combat are analysed in split seconds and tenths-of-seconds.

An interesting side-shoot, between the detective novel and the action thriller proper, is the pure suspense story in which either the murderer, or the victim, but in any case not the detective, is the real hero. Patricia Highsmith (*Strangers on a Train*, 1949; *The Talented Mr Ripley*, 1955) is the best representative of the first category; William Irish (*The Phantom Lady*, 1942; *The Black Angel*, 1943), Boileau and Narcejac (*D'Entre les Morts*, 1956; *A Coeur Perdu*, 1959; *Les Victimes*, 1964) are typical representatives of the second. Boileau and Narcejac have tried to theorize their endeavours. They write:

But one is not a victim because one is hunted and directly

threatened. One becomes a victim as soon as one is present at events whose definitive meaning one is unable to decipher, as soon as the real becomes a trap, as soon as everyday life is turned upside down. One becomes a victim because one seeks vainly for truth, and because the truth one obtains is not the genuine article, and so on and so forth, and the more one thinks rationally the more one goes astray. *The crime story, instead of signalling the triumph of logic, has then to consecrate the failure of rational thought:* it is precisely for this reason that its hero is a victim. (p.178)

This is yet another confirmation of the decline of rationality in bourgeois ideology and society, under the impact of structural crisis, fascism, the authoritarian state and monopoly capitalism. But this first indication of things to come was short-lived, especially because of the economic boom that followed world war two in the West. Boileau and Narcejac note that the vogue for the pure suspense story lasted only four years. Other crises had to occur for irrationality once again to take over the detective story, this time with a vengeance.

Many thriller writers have never succeeded in following up an initial masterpiece. A notable example is Lawrence Sanders, former editor of technological trade journals, who in *The Anderson Tapes* (1970) constructed an impressively gripping suspense story around a super-heist defeated by the new electronic techniques of eavesdropping. Duke Anderson's activities and private life are bugged at every moment by a battery of snooping agencies: the New York Police Department, the Narcotics Board, the Internal Revenue Service, the New York State Income Tax Bureau, Peace of Mind Inc. – a dozen of them in all! Sanders's subsequent novels, however, have been pedestrian and sloppy. Much the same can be said of Trevanian, who has achieved nothing comparable to *Shibumi*, and of Steven King who, after *The Dead Zone* (1979), wrote only horror rubbish.

But this is not the case for the writers one should personally put at the top of the list: Graham Greene, Eric Ambler, John Le Carré, Morris West. Nor, generally speaking for Dick Francis. Nor for Adam Hall's Quiller series, each successive novel as well written and suspenseful as the last. Nor for William Goldman, who has followed up his remarkable *Marathon Man* (1974) with the even more remarkable *Control* (1982), which is about 'travelling clairvoyance' or getting into other people's brains. The literary trick used here is to suggest a simultaneity of events in reality separated by sixty years, then desynchronizing them, while maintaining credibility. *Control* is really a medical thriller like Cook's *Coma* and *Brain*, but with Cold War competition in parapsychology thrown in for good measure. Its indictment of US government wickedness, and its realistic insight into layers of New York society, give the book a depth rarely found in a thriller.

Keeping attention, creating tension, maintaining suspense is a technical craft that imposes its own rules, and that distinguishes efficient detective story, spy novel and thriller authors from unsuccessful ones. One of the tricks of the trade, besides appropriate style and other purely literary requirements, is a subtle mixture of the credible and the incredible, the serious and the lighthearted. A tiny shift, and the balance is broken, credibility lost, suspense gone. We know that no private detective, in real life, will actually dare to induce a murderer to commit suicide, let alone provide the wherewithal to do it. But if the author knows how to work up to that dénouement with each step logically following from the previous one, in a way to make the whole story credible, if the atmosphere created is accepted as realistic, then the credibility of the solution *is* accepted, the plot *isn't* questioned as absurd and the Mad Fascist Billionaire seems to walk out of the pages of *The Times* and not out of an adolescent's day-dream.

But when all is said and done, the suspense story, the spy novel and the thriller, like the detective story, have to do with one thing only: homicide. Murder by bomb, grenade, laser or strafing from the air; murder by side-arm, shotgun, rifle, submachine-gun or bazooka; by poisons and drugs; by strangling, garroting or stoning; by car, by avalanche, or by electrocution; murder by drowning, or by pushing from a height; murder with stick, rock, shoe, scarf, cord or blackjack; murder by piano strings or church bells; murder with fist, hand-chop, and every technique known to the martial arts of Asia; murder by starvation, deprivation of air and light, hypnosis, or terror leading to heart attack; murder by proxy, and by induced suicide; murder by machine, by automaton, by animal agent (hound, crocodile, deadly spider, or in a recent case even a tame boa constrictor!).

We can only shake our heads, sigh, and wonder how tens of millions of devotees can calmly and uncritically *enjoy* reading ten, twenty, thirty episodes of frightful slaughter each year, about five hundred or a thousand imaginary murders in a lifetime. What a terrible society ours must be, what terrible frustrations it must engender, for the description of such acts to be the chosen mode of relaxation and literary pleasure for so many of its members! Even if we were to assume that murder plays a relatively unimportant role in the enjoyment of crime stories, that it is merely a conventional precondition to be fulfilled before the real story begins (as Ernst Bloch alleged): what a terrible society it must still be that so alienates millions of readers of crime stories from reality that they forget, or no longer acknowledge to themselves, that what they are reading about and actually enjoying is that most reprehensible of human actions: the violent suppression of a human life. 'Death seems to provide the minds of the Anglo-Saxon race with a greater fund of innocent enjoyment than any other single subject,' wrote Dorothy Sayers (in *Aristoteles on Detective Fiction*) who knew what she was talking about. Innocent enjoyment of murder – just so.

11. Violence: explosion and implosion

The forties and fifties saw a second watershed in the history of crime in the United States, comparable to that of the twenties: the massive extension of drug addiction and the 'street criminality' linked to it. It has been claimed that between ten and twenty million Americans, most of them young, were involved to some extent by the mid seventies. With some delay, and as yet to a lesser degree, this phenomenon has spread to Western Europe (especially Britain, Italy and France) and to Japan.

The roots of the new development go back to the end of Prohibition. When organized crime lost its bootlegging interests, it could not recoup simply by stepping up its gambling, prostitution and loan-shark operations. What it needed, in place of alcohol, was another consumer good whose distribution, illegal by definition, could be monopolized. Drugs, whose sale even to addicts was forbidden by law, were a natural candidate. By 1938, according to Congressional Representative Coffee, the turnover of drug-peddling in the USA had exceeded one billion dollars a year, the equivalent of six or seven billion in today's terms. Thereafter, a number of social factors were to contribute to a massive further extension of the phenomenon after world war two.

The vast scale of black market operations by GIs in occupied Germany and Japan, and the difficulty for many demobilized soldiers in adapting to civilian life, meant that American cities in the immediate post-war years were thronged with thousands of potential pushers, and tens or hundreds of thousands of demoralized potential users. Then, the great surge of immigration of black and Puerto Rican families into American cities during the war and the post-war boom years; racist discrimination; a school system geared to producing working-class dropouts on a huge scale; and an economic system designed to maintain a permanent reserve army of labour (after the 1949 and 1953 recessions, youth unemployment was between 15 and 20 per cent, rising to 30 per cent and more in the black and hispanic ghettos; these created a massive pool of young people who could find no livelihood other than petty crime. Frank Browning and John Gerassi have argued that this petty criminality – centred around car theft, house-breaking and dope-peddling – forms an integral part of the 'underground' economy that has become a permanent feature of the overall capitalist economy, as entrepreneurs attempt to evade high taxation, social security contributions, and state regulation in general.

On the consumer side, the same psychological stimuli for this massive extension of criminal activity explain the mass explosion of the market for crime and mystery stories: growing frustration and tension in daily life, combined in the case of proletarian and sub-proletarian youth with growing individual despair, lack of any collective social perspective, and a pursuit of all that might distract from the desolate monotony of standardized work, consumption, and welfare. But while preoccupation with crime and violence remains, of course, purely platonic and vicarious for most readers of detective novels, the tenfold multiplication of petty criminals in the big cities of late capitalism led to attempts by the bourgeoisie in many countries, via the mass media and direct political initiatives, to cash in on popular 'fear of violence' to push through repressive and anti-democratic legislation, while blackening the left as permissive and 'soft on violence'.

In actual fact, as Jean-Claude Chesnais (*Histoire de la Violence*, 1981) has convincingly shown, the number of murders and capital crimes is down, not up, in comparison with the late nineteenth and early twentieth centuries, or even with the thirties. This is especially true for Western Europe, thanks to the welfare state and social security; the trend is not surprisingly weakest in the United States, where social security is much lower. In the 1970s the number of homicides per hundred thousand inhabitants was 9.3 in the United States, as against 3 in Finland, 1.4 in Italy, 1.2 in West Germany, 1.1 in Sweden, 1.0 in France, 0.8 in Greece, 0.8 in

Switzerland, and 0.5 in Spain.

The truth is that the trend in major crimes of violence is the reverse of that for petty crime. This clearly shows the ideological function of the great crime scare whipped up by right-wing law-and-order lobbies: systematically to misrepresent the poorest sectors of society and the most exploited layers of the working class as 'criminal classes' prone to mayhem and murder, and thus to justify a systematic strengthening of the repressive apparatus of the state. At the same time, the massive increase in the number of petty criminals was to transform the underworld of organized crime into a hierarchy that, ironically, came ever more faithfully to mirror the structure of the bourgeois world above, with a great mass of pitiful small fry forever in and out of gaol at the bottom, and a handful of monopolists virtually assured of immunity at the top.

It is, however, undeniable that a major explosion of violence did get under way in the United States in the late forties and early fifties, that this gathered momentum throughout the sixties and seventies, that it has tended to spread to most capitalist countries in varying degrees, and that this actual violence matches the general climate of diffused violence in which late capitalist society is increasingly bathed. Growing militarization on the one hand, and children screaming 'I'll run a knife into you' at their mothers or schoolteachers on the other, are just two polar expressions of the same historical trend.

One ominous result of the diffusion of violence has been the upsurge in the number of anonymous, gratuitous, and mass crimes. Whereas, in the thirties, 75 per cent of all New York murders were committed by people who knew their victims, now 75 per cent of homicides are committed by complete strangers. Random mass murders – by the Texas Sniper, Boston Strangler, Son of Sam, Yorkshire Ripper – are ever more frequent. The tragic mass suicide-cum-murder in Guyana of 910 members of the Jim Jones People's Temple sect in November 1978, under the influence of induced paranoia, doubtless represents the most extreme and concentrated expression to date of this tendency to blind violence.

All these trends have a corresponding expression in the evolution of the crime story, of which a sub-species in the forties and fifties veered towards distilled violence and sadism: in France it was dubbed the *série noire* or 'black series'. Typical representatives were Mickey Spillane and James Hadley Chase, with William Irish as precursor, and many French and German (the Jerry Cotton series) followers. What characterized this new offshoot of the traditional detective novel was its greater preoccupation with violence than with the unravelling of any mystery: the mystery often became a mere pretext or vanished altogether. Violence, brutality, cruelty, sadism, maiming and killing for their own sake, became the main subject of the genre, as exemplified most vividly in Chase's *No Orchids for Miss Blandish*. The fact that such novels enjoyed tremendous success clearly confirms their status as reflections of a sick society: they were phenomena of social decomposition. (Contrary to what many people believe, Chase was in fact English, not American: as Benvenuti and Rizzoni point out, his precursor was Peter Cheyney of Lemmy Caution fame, although Cheyney's novels were not themselves as imbued with violence as those of the true *série noire*. Mickey Spillane and his hero Mike Hammer, however, were one-hundred-per-cent American.)

The brutality and sadism of the *série noire* coincided with a real literary decline. This can be attributed to the new stage reached by mass production in the field of authorship, the development of conveyor-belt techniques, often based on the use of ghost writers. Chase is said to have written *No Orchids for Miss Blandish* in six weeks flat. Many titles in the Jerry Cotton series are said to have been written by students, for as little as $300 per book, by cannibalizing previous books in the series and reconstituting selected ingredients around a new central idea furnished by the publishing house.

This regression in technique opened the way for deeper changes. The new crudity and directness of language made possible a change in the nature of the medium itself. Just as the hard-boiled 'action' novel had originally evolved from pulp-magazine series of the Nick Carter or Black Mask type, so now the *série noire* story of violence reverted to a comic-strip universe of simplistic (and sadistic) Manichaeanism. Then, of course, from that comic-strip universe to actual comics (of which the Dick Tracy series represented a still relatively honourable prototype) was a short step. Pulp writing led to an increasing absorption of the entire sub-genre into comic magazines.

But one must be prepared for the occasional surprise. In Mexico, I came across a comic-strip series featuring the character of Fantomas in a new set of contemporary adventures: one of these involved a quite exciting and class-conscious sortie into the Poland of Lech Walesa, to mobilize workers in the factories and on the streets behind the banner of Solidarność!

This, of course, is exceptional. As a general rule, the elimination of reasoning, of subtleties of plot, and often of any element of mystery, in favour of violent action pure and simple, means that the comic-strip heirs of the *série noire* are explicitly and rabidly reactionary. It is no exaggeration to speak of a pre-fascist or semi-fascist ideology that often merges with various forms of mysticism, occultism, devil-cults and so on. That this should have been the final destination of the *série noire* was, moreover, no accident. The voice of inhumanity already came through loud and clear in the novels of Mickey Spillane: 'Go after the big boys. Oh, don't arrest them, don't treat them to the democratic processes of courts and law ... do the same thing to them that they'd do to you! Treat 'em to the unglorious taste of sudden death ... Kill 'em left and right, show 'em that we aren't so soft after all. Kill, kill, kill, kill!' (Quoted by Pete Hamill, 'Mike and Mickey', in Dilys Winn, *Murder Ink*, p.132.)

It should be stressed that the decline of reason and rationality in the comics spawned by the *série noire* was not simply a question of content; it was also a question of the form itself. The gradual replacement of a written culture by a sub-culture of techno-imagination and increasing illiteracy undoubtedly constitutes a formal expression of cultural decline, corresponding in its own way to the decline of bourgeois society and the threat of a decline of civilization itself. While third-world countries are struggling to eliminate illiteracy, in the West there is a growing, albeit still marginal, loss of knowledge of the written language, testified to by a number of empirical studies, like those carried out among American, British, and French soldiers.

Even if an excessive simplification and standardization of

language teaching methods (the substitution of mechanical questions-and-answers for the systematic building up of an understanding of context: syntax, grammar, analysis of the structure of language) have contributed to the decline, it remains the case that the replacement of books by comics and television is really a crucial factor. Specialists in the science of communications are increasingly coming to argue that the replacement of written texts by images, of transparent linearity by opaque space, almost inevitably leads to more primitive content, acts regressively upon the content of communication itself. (Thus the information that there are now more video shops in Britain than bookshops – *Sunday Times*, 8 August 1982 – is disturbing.) Mental structures themselves become involved in the change. Historical thought; deductive and dialectical thought; inductive, causal and scientific thought: all are structurally linked to the written word. A reversal to non-written language, to what are essentially more primitive forms of communication, must stimulate pre-logical, ahistorical, and indeed anti-historical, more and more primitive forms of thinking as well. The regression represented by the *série noire* and its comic-strip heirs, suffused as they are with an inhuman sadism and preoccupied with the most repellent forms of human behaviour, strikingly bears out the correctness of this hypothesis.

12. From crime to business

The growth of organized crime raised the problem of finding outlets for the accumulated gains. In a capitalist society, any sizeable sum of money not spent on current consumption will tend to transform itself into capital, to bear interest, and to participate in the general distribution of social surplus-value. Big-time gangsters have usually been big-time spenders. But during the twenties and thirties their income grew much more quickly than their expenditure, so a growing problem of investment arose. This problem became really explosive in the forties and fifties, when organized crime became centred around drug traffic, and its profits rose dramatically. By 1978, the crime syndicate's annual turnover in the United States was estimated at some $62 billion (Charlier and Marcilly, p.10), and criminal profits are now regularly assessed by *Business Week*, as part of the hidden economy.

Capital accumulated through crime first moved into the New York garment industry, before spreading out to greener pastures. The first targets were entertainment, gambling, tourism, luxury hotels – not just in Las Vegas or Atlantic City, but also, for instance, in Batista's Havana. Here, the dividing line was still fluid between actual crime (prostitution, illegal gambling, protection) and legitimate business. But the bigger the takings became, the larger loomed the problem of reinvesting them securely and maintaining regular cash flows. The inner logic of money-capital accumulation took over from that of monopolizing criminal activities. A dual obsession took hold of the big-time gangsters moving into this new dimension: how to 'launder' their ill-gotten gains, as a precondition for their introduction into the circuit of 'normal' capital accumulation; and how themselves to enter branches of 'normal' economic activity (production, transport, distribution, finance) where alone continuously enlarged reproduction of capital is possible. The single formula is still 'to go legit'.

The move into legitimate business was usually linked to activities already penetrated by the syndicate for criminal purposes: public works and the construction industry; trucking; real estate; branches of textiles; night-clubs; brewing and distilling; importing and exporting; distribution; professional sport; shipping; second-hand cars; slot-machine operations, and perhaps manufacturing. But these sectors were still marginal, and did not involve big business proper. Things really changed when the syndicate began to take over local banks, moved into the investment-trust business (as when Vesco bought up IOS), dabbled in currency speculation and the movement of gold and silver, got a finger into such diverse pies as the futures market and agrobusiness, and in general attempted to ride the great wave of speculation unleashed by the breakdown of the Bretton Woods international monetary system in the early seventies.

The success of the big gangsters in going legit can be gauged by their personal capital accumulation which reached astronomic proportions. The US business fortnightly *Forbes* has started to publish a regular list of the 400 richest families in the country. The first of these (13 September 1982) included at least three families of avowed gangsters among the greatest fortunes of North America. Meyer Lansky, one of the original organizers of the syndicate, in which he was probably second only to Lucky Luciano, was eighth on the list, with an estimated $1.5 billion. He was preceded only by the Ludwig, Getty, du Pont, Rockefeller, Hunt, Annenberg, and Hewlett families and preceded such renowned monopolists as the Morgans, the (IBM) Watsons, the Loebs, the Mellons, and the Deeres. The syndicate family of Morris Dalitz is also said by *Forbes* to figure among the Four Hundred, together with associate Robert Vesco. The relations of Joseph Kennedy with organized crime in the Prohibition period are common knowledge.

A decade after the syndicate's breakthrough into legitimate business in the United States, a similar development took place in Italy. In the immediate post-war period, the Mafia was still centred around powerful landowners. Its political links with the local and regional bosses of Christian Democracy had primarily served to suppress or weaken the unionization of agricultural labourers, and to prevent the organization of poor farmers. But from the early sixties on, major economic changes were to occur. Large-scale state investment flowed into southern Italy and Sicily. The relative weight of agriculture declined, that of industry rose. To cash in on the bonanza, the Sicilian Mafia moved the bulk of its operations from the countryside to the city.

Now the Mafia took over key sectors of the house- and road-building industries, sub-contracting in the automobile and steel industries, the manufacture and distribution of spare parts, the port of Palermo, and all aspects of food distribution in the city. All this was achieved through 'normal' monopolistic business practice (the pressure of large-scale capital accumulation), political pressure (patronage and graft), and outright criminal activity (extortion, racketeering, take-over by intimidation or actual assassination). The Mafia set up a full-scale regional power structure, which it controlled with an iron hand. To enforce its rule, it carried out at least thirty sensational murders of political opponents, from the Palermo prosecutors Scaglione (1971) and Costa, to the federal secretary of the Communist Party in Palermo, Pio La Torre, to General Della Chiesa (1982), chief of Carabinieri and newly appointed prefect of Palermo, who had just been entrusted by the Rome government with the task of heading the struggle against the Sicilian Mafia.

Estimates of the annual revenues of the Mafia nationally vary. A major part, of course, is derived from narcotics, since following the destruction of the 'French Connection' Italy once again became the principal *entrepôt* for drug traffic between Asia and the Middle East, and Britain and North America. *Il Mondo* and *Der Spiegel* (13 September 1982) estimated the total annual turnover of organized crime in Italy at $12 billion, nearly half of it coming from narcotics. Some 80 per cent of the 200,000 employees in the Sicilian construction industry are said to be on the Mafia's payroll.

The biggest problem for the Mafia, as it was a generation earlier for the American Syndicate, was laundering dirty money. The Sindona group, which crashed during the 1974–75 recession, and later the Banco Ambrosiano, which met the same fate in the crisis of 1980–82, apparently provided some of the main avenues for this. So we can see how the profits of big crime, once it has to infiltrate big capital, become vulnerable to capitalist crises just like those of any 'normal' business. At all events, there is no doubt that for the Mafia going legit meant, among other things, going into banking. Over the past twenty years, the number of banking agencies throughout Italy has increased by 83 per cent; in Sicily, however, it has increased by 586 per cent (*Le Matin*, 7 September 1982). Today, of the 383 Sicilian municipalities, only 66 do not have at least one such agency.

Apart from banking, one of the most important means whereby organized crime in all countries launders illegal money is through the traffic in stolen or counterfeit stocks and shares: official sources (quoted by Hougan, p.210) give a figure of $50 billion for the total value of stolen stocks and shares circulating in the United States. However, banking remains the key. Entire banks have been set up to serve the interests of Syndicate financiers like Lansky. Indeed, according to Hougan (who quotes several sources), even the most powerful bank in the Middle East prior to the 1973 oil boom, Lebanon's Intra Bank, which collapsed in 1967, was said to have been heavily involved in the laundering business; it also controlled the Casino du Liban, whose manager Marcel-Paul Francisi (of Corsican/French Connection fame) is said to have been one of the bosses of the Middle-East drug trade.

The infiltration of organized crime into 'legitimate' big business – or their mutual interpenetration – not surprisingly exercises a powerful fascination upon a wide public, providing a strong motive for writers to introduce it as a theme around which to construct their plots. Strangely enough, though there has been a proliferation of movies about gangsters going legit, the last decades of the Syndicate's evolution have left fewer romanticized literary records than earlier ones. A few novels come to mind – Philip Loraine's *A Mafia Kiss* (1969), or Donald Westlake's *The Busy Body* (1966) and *Cops and Robbers* (1972). A fairly good description of middle-level Mafia operations can be found in John D. MacDonald's *The Scarlet Ruse* (1974). It is little enough.

But there has been an outcrop of new anti-Mafia stories of the crude 'pulp magazine' type. The first of these was perhaps Don

Pendleton's *War Against the Mafia* (1969), a book that gave rise to a whole new variety of *série noire*, sadistic avenger stories. (In *The Penetrator*, the hero, predictably, actually penetrates the Mafia.) The best, or least bad of this anti-Mafia school have been the Executioner series, the Matt Helm series, and *The Violent World of Parker* (Westlake). A comic parody should also be mentioned: Jimmy Breslin's *The Gang that Couldn't Shoot Straight* (1970).

The main attempt to cash in on the wave of public interest, however, has involved purportedly true-life 'revelations' rather than fictional thrillers. Among these, one may single out Peter Maas's *The Valachi Papers* (1969) and *Serpico* (1973), Martin and Hammel Gosch's *The Last Testament of Lucky Luciano*, Vito Genovese's *Memoirs*, and Mario Puzo's *The Godfather* (1969). (These have been accompanied by a growing list of historical works about the Mafia: to quote just a few, Mario Farinella and Felice Chilanti, *Rapporto sulla Mafia* (1964), Norman Lewis, *The Honoured Society* (1964), Emanuele Macaluso, *La Mafia e lo Stato* (1971), Gaetano Falzone, *Histoire de la Mafia* (1973), Gaia Servadio, *Mafioso: a History of the Mafia from its Origins to the Present Day* (1976).)

Puzo's *Godfather* is really a category of its own. The author had earlier demonstrated a critical social consciousness, in his efforts to stigmatize – in an almost Swiftian manner – the resemblances between bourgeois society and the criminal establishment in the United States. One of his first essays bore the title: 'How crime keeps America healthy, wealthy, cleaner and more beautiful.' In another he wrote:

> How are we to adjust to a society that drafts human beings to fight a war, yet permits its businessmen to make a profit from the shedding of blood?... as society becomes more and more criminal, the well-adjusted citizen, by definition, must become more and more criminal. So let us now dare to take the final step. (Puzo, p.79)

The final step was to present the top American criminal as the best-adjusted American citizen.

However, as John Sutherland has reminded us, Puzo himself

said that he wrote *The Godfather* just to make money. For him it was a conscious sellout (which shows that he had not entirely lost his social awareness, or at least his sense of guilt about that sellout): 'I was forty-five years old and tired of being an artist ... It was time to grow up and sell out.' (Puzo, p.34) Swiftian irony is not what makes a best seller these days. The irony in *The Godfather* became so subtle that 99 per cent of its millions of readers have certainly been quite unaware of it. By a dialectical twist (Hegel's *List der Geschichte*), the true irony (or inner logic of the story?) lay in the fact that the book shaped up into a real apology for the Mafia. The *capo dei tutti capi* is an exemplary family man, who protects his friends, makes people happy, is a great one for charity and philanthropy, manifests every sterling virtue and is a model citizen. If he has a few enemies killed, their number is insignificant compared to those eliminated by the President of the United States, the Judiciary, the Chiefs of Staff of the Armed Forces, or Big Business. So why should the poor man be treated as a fall guy? Is he not rather a victim of racist prejudice against Italian-Americans?

Perhaps, in the final analysis, the declining importance of gangsters and of the theme of mobsters going legit in the evolution of the crime story can be explained by the fact that organized crime – especially after its transformation into another form of big business – ceases to offer much in the way of mystery. Its crimes are no longer covered up, or barely so. Its murders are signed, in the United States as much as in Sicily. It seems to have nothing to hide; its responsibility is public knowledge. So the problem ceases to be the criminological one of investigating a crime, and identifying a murderer; instead, it becomes the politico-economic one of securing conviction and breaking up a powerful organization. What is needed is not a study of clues, but a destruction of well-established links between the Syndicate and the local, regional, and national capitalist power structure. It should not be forgotten that even Al Capone was convicted only of tax evasion, not of murder. When the rules of capital accumulation come to guide the behaviour of organized crime, it is hardly surprising that they should increasingly come to share a common scale of values with society at large. As one Mafia boss says to an ex-associate in a famous story: 'Gloria, what did you do? You interfered with business.'

The more highly organized crime becomes, the more murder changes its very nature. Consequently, it cannot remain the only, or even the main, subject of the crime novel. It can only undergo a transformation in literary discourse similar to what it undergoes in real life. Murder, as a product of love, hate, envy, jealousy, malice, greed, or blackmail, disappears or slips back to the periphery of criminal activity. Members of the Syndicate have no right to threaten the corporate interest for reasons of individual passion. The individual criminal has as little place in the Syndicate's universe as the independent craftworker has in the multinational corporation. Only the Organization has the right to wreak vengeance – in its own interests, for the sake of its own security, and to its own greater glory. In the world of corporate crime, only murder for the Organization's sake retains citizenship rights. But this means that only one fundamental motive survives for murder: greed, or the pursuit of the Syndicate's material and security interests. Murder becomes anonymous in the strictest sense, an anonymous business: Murder, Inc.

In this way, corporate crime reduces murder to a pure instrument of profit: hardly surprising, since profit is the common link between capitalism as a system, business activity and organized crime. The wages of sin may be death, but the wages of organized crime are capital accumulation. Organized crime is capitalism freed from the bonds of penal law, but accepting most of the civil and certainly the commercial code. Its particular mode of alienation leads to murder for business, to the business of murder as a pure source of profit, to, as it were, disembodied murder, to the doubly alienated murderer, the murderer without personal involvement or passion, the murderer for pure profit. The hired Mafia killer steps into the shoes of the jealous lover, the scheming debtor, or the blackmailed doctor. The killer is a professional, an expert, a technician of crime, on a par with the specialist in space technology, production schedules, business administration, or electoral campaigning. Murder thus loses its mysterious qualities, its exotic flavour. It no longer stalks at night, for sunlight is no longer a threat. Everyone now knows 'whodunit', or, rather, knowing who has had it done, has ceased to care who has actually pulled the trigger. The only open question is whether the contract will be fulfilled. Here again, language is revealing: with the concept of 'contract', murder proclaims loud and clear its common ground with general commercial practice, motivated by the pursuit of profit.

13. From business to crime

Late capitalism is characterized by a tremendous extension of state intervention in the economic field, and a concomitant hypertrophy of the state and para-state apparatus. This implies a no less impressive extension of the battery of laws, decrees, ordinances and regulations that confront the individual entrepreneur or single corporation. This mountain of laws is less and less respected in everyday life.

In the first place, for objective reasons. It has become practically impossible to observe or respect such a mass of legal provisions, sometimes even to be aware of them. Some provisions contradict others. The choice facing business people and companies is then which laws to circumvent or violate, rather than whether to violate or respect the law.

In the second place, the hypertrophy of the state implies a hypertrophy of taxation. Though an increasing proportion of taxes – the bulk of them, both direct and indirect, in most Western countries – are paid by wage and salary-earners rather than by capitalists, this circumstance does not prevent the individual entrepreneur, company, or *rentier* from considering increases in their taxation intolerable. A striking contradiction, with significance for the entire epoch of bourgeois dominance, now sharpens rapidly: that between the interests of the single firm, as the basic cell of the capitalist mode of production, and the interests of the mode of production in its totality. Individual capitalists see themselves as taxpayers, and wish to reduce taxation to the utmost. The capitalist mode of production as a whole, however, needs to expand taxation in order to function more efficiently in a period of growing economic, social, military and political tension. The result is that tax evasion and fraud become a primary preoccupation of the bourgeois class. A whole new profession springs up, the fiscal advisers whose function it is to ensure by hook or by crook that their clients pay less tax than they should, and if possible none at all. Loopholes in the law are exploited, and foreign tax havens proliferate. Places like the Isle of Man or the Channel Islands, even whole countries like Luxembourg, Liechtenstein, Andorra, Monaco, the Caymans and the Bahamas owe a significant part of their global revenues to this function.

In the third place, employer associations, trade associations, chambers of commerce and, above all, large corporations employ lobbies to manipulate the framing and practical application of laws intended to regulate business activity in specific fields or branches of industry, so as to favour rather than restrict the freedom of corporations to fleece consumers, deny citizens a real choice, or restrain competitors from threatening their profits. The activity of these lobbies requires the systematic corruption of legislators and state functionaries, as was strikingly confirmed by the Abscam operation mounted by the FBI.

In the fourth place, US capital exports after world war two underwent a qualitative growth, and subsequently the same became true for the foreign operations of West German, Japanese and Italian multinational corporations (British, French, Dutch, Belgian, Swiss and Portuguese capitalists already had experience in this domain dating back to the pre-war period). Such foreign operations brought the multinationals into contact with societies in which average incomes at every level, and the resources available to individual local companies, politicians, and high state function-aries, were so much inferior to those prevailing in their parent countries, that the temptation to use bribery, corruption, and financial blackmail on an ever-increasing scale became virtually irresistible. The differences in question existed not just between imperialist countries and the third world, but also between the richer and poorer imperialist countries; witness the best-known recent case of multinational corruption, the Lockheed scandal.

The whole issue became so important in the United States that a Congressional inquiry was held on it, leading to the adoption of the Corrupt Practices Act of 1977. It also spawned books. One with the eloquent title *Bribery and Extortion in World Business*, by Neil H. Jacoby, Peter Nehemkis and Richard Eels, gives the following succinct exposition of the illegal means utilized by contemporary business circles:

> The revelations that several hundred major American business corporations made payments for political influence and special favors to foreign political figures and government employees were hardly news to knowledgeable people in business, in politics, in the news media, and, one must assume, in the Securities and Exchange Commission itself. Indeed, here in the United States, corruption in business-government relations has been fairly common for a long time. (p. 172) ... Political payments are institutionalized facts in international business. In almost every country in which they have ventured as investors or traders, American businessmen have encountered the phenomenon of the pay-off – the practice of bribing government officials as a condition of doing business, government employees extorting money as a condition of the performance of their official duties, government employees expecting – indeed demanding – kickbacks in contracts awarded in performance of their discretionary power, politicians extracting campaign contributions for their parties and campaigns, frequently under duress or threats to the security of the investments. (p. 4) ... Politicians 'on the take' generally designate a numbered Swiss bank account as the depository for a payment, although Japanese politicians seem to prefer to be paid in yen and to receive funds directly. In making a payment to the former Honduran President-General, Oswaldo Lopez Arellano, United Brands deposited $1.25 million in a numbered Swiss bank account. (p. 6)

Four hundred US firms in all, including one third of the 500 biggest, admitted having paid out $750 million in bribes in the 1973-78 period.

In the fifth place, the enhanced role of the state sector in the economy, through the increased purchase of goods and services by state bodies – above all the armed forces, but also public corporations in such sectors as telecommunications, mass transport, energy, etc. – similarly augments the temptation for large companies and rich individual business people to use their immense financial resources to improve their chances of securing orders, or to push up their share of the public-sector market. The result is a systematic use of corruption and blackmail, to an extent quite unknown in the past.

Finally, in the course of capitalist competition itself, the concentration and centralization of capital have reached such a pitch in the epoch of monopoly capital that the way has been opened for huge resources to be used illegally: secret cartels, collusive arrangements designed to impose higher prices (the most prominent recent case was that of the US electrical-equipment monopolies, which culminated in a famous trial in 1960-61); fraudulent operations such as the oil companies' attempt in 1973-74 to declare previous stocks as current production; industrial espionage; slashing the quality of products sold to the public, without any corresponding cut in price; and so on. Indeed, these practices became so widespread that a new concept was coined to describe them (apparently by the criminologist Edwin Sutherland): 'white collar crime' (the German equivalent is *Wirtschaftsverbrechen*). A study published in 1977 by the American Management Association, *Crimes Against Business*, estimated the annual fruits of such white collar delinquency at $30-40 billion. According to Ralph Nader's research group in the US, at the start of the seventies the annual cost to the American public of illegal monopolist practices amounted to between forty-eight and sixty billion dollars: this figure was higher even than the total annual turnover of organized crime in the United States.

The upshot of all the changes enumerated above implies a radical change in the behaviour of the individual bourgeois and the single corporation towards their own state and law. The lament of the French bourgeois politician Odilon Barrot under the July Monarchy, on the eve of the 1848 revolution – 'Legality is stifling us' – is increasingly becoming the cry of contemporary business. It tends less and less to take respect for the law for granted. It becomes more and more obsessed by the need to transgress that law in the course of everyday practice. Illegality replaces legality as the normal framework of commercial, industrial and financial behaviour.

One by-product of this change has been a constant expansion of the legal profession, itself increasingly organized on the basis of commercial firms. Large corporations employ dozens of lawyers, whose prime function is to negotiate with state officials, competitors, clients, suppliers and legal antagonists. By persuading them to drop lawsuits or threatening them with litigation themselves (inevitably lengthy and costly) – in effect, by blackmailing them – they can raise the corporation's profits and reduce its losses. Such negotiations are extended to the sphere of the judiciary itself, where an ever higher percentage of cases are settled out of court. The very growth of litigation can only lead in this direction. According to *Le Monde* (31 October 1982), the number of civil cases brought before French tribunals rose from 439,677 in 1970 to 733,879 in 1980, while the number of reports (*procès-verbaux*) remitted to the public prosecutor rose in the same period from 9,878,403 to 15,368,661 per annum (15 million per annum for a population of less than 55 million!).

All these momentous transformations at the level of practice could not but exercise profound influence at the level of predominant bourgeois ideology, whose privileged expression in the field of literature is the crime story. There has been a steady increase in the number of thrillers in which the use of criminal methods by big business is portrayed in great detail (for the most part, but by no means invariably, with negative connotations). In 1959 William Haggard was already impressively outlining in *The Teleman Touch* the shady, indeed openly criminal, activities of large oil companies. These have since figured as the villains in quite a number of other thrillers, among them Alistair MacLean's *Sea Witch* (1977). In Jeffrey Archer's *Shall We Tell the President?* (1977), the US small-arms industry plans to murder the president, with the connivance of a blackmailed senator, in order to prevent the passing of a bill restricting the private sale of guns. A drug company's illegal dealings in Africa provides the subject for Robert McCrum's *A Loss of Heart* (1982). After Ian Fleming's death John Gardner wrote a sequel to the Bond series, *Licence Renewed* (1981), that featured a crooked tycoon with vast interests in electronics, aviation and nuclear power. A chemical trust's illegal pollution is indicted in Robin Cook's *Fever* (1982). In *Basikasingo* (1982), John Matthews depicts the diamond cartel itself, from its supreme chief down (is there no law against libel?) as engaging in criminal activities to secure its position. Rival tycoons employ still more criminal means, including large-scale theft and multiple murder, in their attempts to take the place of the cartel's boss. Similarly, banks or other financial institutions have figured as the main villains in a number of thrillers.

All these books share a common defect, however, that keeps them within the framework of bourgeois ideology. While individual giant corporations, or even by implication all such organizations, are indeed indicted, sometimes in terms sharper than many Marxists would use, the overall system never is. Yet it is the capitalist system that has spawned these corporations, and that will reproduce them again and again, even if they are occasionally prosecuted for their crimes or even more infrequently allowed to go bankrupt. The truth is that, together, they are the system. So how can one condemn all the parts, while upholding the whole? Is it a question of blindness, naivety, cynicism, or outright material self-interest? Successful crime-story writers are, after all, part of the bourgeois class, albeit not at the exalted level of the multinational corporations and their bosses.

14. State, business and crime

The massive expansion of crime in advanced capitalist countries, first (in the United States) as a consequence of Prohibition, later, thanks to the world-wide extension of the drugs traffic and of organized criminal syndicates, has created specific problems for law enforcement. The borderline between law enforcement and crime prevention became increasingly blurred as the collection of information moved towards the centre of police operations. The very nature of mass crime and violence as 'blind' and anonymous ensured that informing would become a key aspect of the uncovering of culprits. The police could no longer operate without constant recourse to informers and stool-pigeons. Popular American television series such as *Kojak* and *Starsky and Hutch* have had the merit of offering visual proof, so to speak, of the new set-up: the stool-pigeon organically integrated into the camp of the righteous defenders of law and order.

But the change does not stop there. Informers cannot fulfil their function without entering into a delicate game of *do ut des*. Information flows in two directions: from the criminal milieu to the police, and from the authorities to the underworld. Some crimes are solved or prevented only because others are allowed to take place or to remain undiscovered. Thus a symbiosis arises between the two sides of the law, and this symbiosis creates moral ambiguity and material corruption. Not just information, but money too flows in both directions. Informers grow rich by betraying their former associates; police grow rich by letting certain gangsters off the hook, for the sake of arresting others.

In recent years this phenomenon has attained astonishing dimensions, as the Valachi and Serpico cases in the United States have shown. Leaving aside the complex question of the degree of individual corruption among the police, let us concentrate rather on the social aspect of the problem. It has become more and more impossible to fight organized crime without tolerating and indeed actually favouring organized crime, both by the methods used and by the results achieved. The drugs traffic provides an excellent illustration of this.

The reason is obvious. Organized crime, rather than being peripheral to bourgeois society, springs increasingly from the same socio-economic motive forces that govern capital accumulation in general: private property, competition and generalized commodity production (generalized money economy). The Swedish pop group Abba summed up the situation eloquently in their song: 'Money, money, money — It's a rich man's world.' (Their own fate is a vivid illustration of this law: with the huge income generated by their records they promptly created an investment trust, and contributed on a large scale to the election funds of the bourgeois party coalition.) But a rich man's world is also a rich gangster's world, particularly since the top gangsters have grown richer and richer in relative terms, and are certainly qualitatively richer than even the richest police, or the overwhelming mass of politicians. (Nixon himself was conscious of the disparity.)

The key economic problem for organized crime, as we have seen, was to find legitimate outlets for illegally accumulated capital. Under late capitalism, this is merely a specific – perhaps paradoxical, even grotesque – reflection of a more general problem: that of finding adequate fields of investment for masses of surplus capital. The two phenomena, however, do not simply dovetail; they actually tend to flow into each other and interpenetrate. Dirty money is laundered through bank deposits located – often, though not solely – in tax havens. But the legitimate equivalent of hot money – surplus capital – tends likewise to find its way to the same banks in the same tax havens. Dirty and clean funds intermingle in balance sheets. They also intermingle in the practical pursuit of surplus-value, by every means possible.

The borderline separating unscrupulous speculators, confidence-tricksters operating on a grand scale in the field of legitimate business, and outright crooks, is becoming thinner and thinner. Investors' Overseas Services (IOS) was a case in point. Barny Cornfield started his gigantic confidence trick, not as an outright swindler, but as an adventurous speculator imprudently extrapolating post-war boom trends into a limitless future. This misjudgement cost his naive collaborators and investors millions of dollars, out of the almost two billion dollars' worth of deposits that he collected. Worse was to come, however: an outright crook, Robert Vesco, took over and simply stole $224 million, which he then held onto with the complicity of the highest authorities in a number of countries, beginning with the Bahamas and Costa Rica.

Other crooks were enabled to operate only by the cover that the highest authorities in the United States itself provided. In the sixties, a Texan entrepreneur managed to pile up $20 million through dealings in fictitious fertilizer stocks, skilfully exploiting the greed of private capitalists and the intricacies of bourgeois state legislation. Shortly afterwards, a group of brilliant young operators set up Equity Funding Inc., whose annual reports declared that it had invested bonds worth $20 million in a Midwest bank, and further millions of dollars in mutual funds (unit trusts): the truth was that Equity Funding had never either possessed any bonds or loaned anything to mutual funds (Raymond Dirks and Leonard Gross, *The Great Wall Street Scandal*).

Things do not function in any fundamentally different way where certain key state activities are concerned. As it has carried out its role of protecting, expanding and sustaining the foreign operations of US corporations and the world-wide interests of US capitalism, the American state has had to create successive agencies for covert action on an international level: first the OSS, then the CIA (whose first director, significantly enough, was a banker and brother to a Secretary of State). A whole library of books has been published about the illegal or actually criminal operations mounted in foreign countries by these bodies, with many of the most telling revelations originating from former CIA agents themselves. The infiltration of informers into the most varied organizations – from cultural associations and student bodies to trade-union federations and rival intelligence agencies – goes hand in hand with, on the one hand, a systematic use of corruption and, on the other, direct recourse to crime, up to and including murder. Torturers are trained, military coups are prepared and organized, and govern-ments considered insufficiently friendly to US capital or having had the audacity to nationalize American-owned firms are systematically subverted. Sometimes such operations are planned and executed jointly with the firms involved, as in the case of the ITT conspiracy with CIA and Pentagon assistance against the legitimate government of Salvador Allende in Chile.

Inside the United States and other Western countries, political police agencies like the FBI are similarly engaged in the large-scale infiltration of organizations seen as hostile to bourgeois society, often without any legal authorization or justification. The widespread use of informers, phone-tapping, bribery, perjury, and similar shady or criminal activities; the granting of official pardons for avowed crimes; indulgence towards right-wing terrorism and anti-union violence to the point of actual cover-ups: all these form part of the arsenal at the disposal of the contemporary state apparatus.

It sometimes happens that the symbiosis between the organs of the state, big business and organized crime is suddenly revealed by some particular incident, such as the abortive Bay of Pigs operation mounted against the Cuban revolution, in which the CIA, the US government (both the Eisenhower and Kennedy administrations), and the Mafia were all involved. (There have been persistent rumours concerning the possible connection between these events and the assassination of President Kennedy.)

An identical symbiosis was illustrated by the notorious case of the SAC in France. This was initially a private police utilized by the Gaullists in their struggle against the OAS, in the last stages and immediate aftermath of the Algerian War. Later it became the Gaullists' secret army for use against political enemies of every kind. Finally it degenerated into a gang of simple racketeers, who established a long and bloody record of violence, torture and murder. In the end, after Mitterrand came to power and following a devastating parliamentary report in the wake of the execution of a local SAC leader and his entire family (seven persons in all!) in the Midi, the SAC was at last officially dissolved.

But the most revealing single instance to date of this growing symbiosis between organized crime, big business, and the state was the one that bound together the Banco Ambrosiano, the Mafia, and the Italian and Vatican states. When the Banco Ambrosiano cracked, leaving a $1.7 billion hole, it was revealed that the bank's chief executive, Roberto Calvi, had been closely connected with the crooked banker Sindona, whose banks had crashed in both Europe and the United States in 1975. Sindona was linked both to top Italian business circles, whose members he had helped to evade taxes and export capital illegally, and to the Mafia. Both Sindona and Calvi had close relations with factions in the Vatican and among Christian Democrat politicians. In fact, the principal Vatican bank, *Istituto per le Opere di Religione* (IOR) had given provisional guarantees to certain operations of the Banco Ambrosiano in Central America involving IOR-controlled companies in Panama, operations that may have been a cover for huge illegal transfers of capital and speculative activities. Public surprise climaxed when it was learnt that Archbishop Marcinkus, head of the IOR, had been interrogated at length by the FBI in 1977 for alleged links with the Mafia, who presumably wanted to use the extra-territorial facilities of the Vatican bank in Italy to launder dirty money, just as many of the richest Italian families turned to those same facilities for purposes of tax evasion and capital export.[1]

This episode was only the latest and most dramatic in a whole series reflecting the links between Italian political or economic life and organized crime. The role played by the billion-dollar traffic in illegal arms in cementing relations between local Christian Democrat factions and the Mafia in Sicily is well known. In the Italian south the Red Brigades now seem to have joined the unholy alliance between Christian Democrat local bosses and the gangsters of the Camorra, claiming, in pseudo-Marxist formulae, that social movements mobilized by these forces represent a 'just struggle of the super-exploited sub-proletariat': the millionaire racketeers of the Camorra a 'sub-proletariat' – isn't that a bit thick?

Finally, what is one to say of the persistent and reliable reports according to which a key source of the world's heroin supply – the so-called Golden Triangle, on the borders of Burma, Thailand, Laos and China – was for a time at least partly controlled by the CIA (together with the transport network which took the drug to the Middle East, Europe and the United States)? On the other side of the world, too, in countries like Bolivia, Peru and Colombia, illegal drugs top the league of exports. *Los narco-traficantes* control military and political personnel at the highest levels, including, until recently in Bolivia, the President of the Republic, General Garcia Meza. And when officials of the US drugs enforcement agency clash with these highly placed gangsters, a welter of patriotic rhetoric is unleashed about the need to defend 'national resources' from Yankee imperialism!

The important thing to emphasize is that the secret of that growing symbiosis does not lie in any obscure, Satanic conspiracy, or in an innately evil human nature. It lies rather in the all-pervasive power of big money, its magnetic capacity under generalized commodity production to attract more money and more power (surplus-value, and a growing lien on the state). Do away with the institutions of market economy, and the symbiosis will disappear. Suppress them only in part, and crime, corruption, greed and the power of money will half-disappear, half-survive among bureaucrats. This is precisely what has occurred in the Soviet Union, China and Eastern Europe (where the crime novel too has partly disappeared and partly survived – but that is another story).[2]

Perhaps the best illustration of how far this symbiosis of state, big business, and crime has gone is provided by the phenomenon of 'spooks'. These are former government or military intelligence agents who set up private 'security' businesses to further the interests of private corporations or wealthy individuals (including gangsters), often by illegal or downright criminal means. Since they are often used for 'dirty tricks' by official security agencies like the FBI or CIA, SAS or MI5, the borderline between spooks and actual government agents is never clearly drawn, as the Watergate scandal dramatically showed.

The tremendous expansion of the security 'community' in the United States during and after world war two was the most immediate source of this phenomenon. The community may have involved as many as half a million agents or collaborators, which means that the number of former intelligence personnel released by natural turnover and periodic conjunctural purges (such as occurred after Watergate) was huge. Since it is possible to survive in capitalist society only by selling one's labour power (unless one happens to be rich), since labour power is determined partly by skill, and since the only skill secret agents generally possess is what can be euphemistically repackaged as 'security services', it was virtually inevitable that a large private security network should have been spawned by the vast intelligence apparatus of the state.

Meanwhile, demand developed at the same rate as supply. The world-wide operations of the multinationals brought them face to face with governments, public officials and state agencies, whether in collision or collusion. The immense stakes of monopolistic competition increased with the wealth and power of the giant corporations themselves. And the explosion of electronic know-how created a real arsenal for industrial and financial crime. So it is hardly surprising that there should have arisen a virtually unlimited demand for such services as surveillance, bugging, wire-tapping, industrial espionage and theft, the milking of electronic data (and sometimes the funds controlled by these), even outright murder.

Jim Hougan's *Spooks* (1978) describes a number of well-known and not-so-well-known international scandals that illustrate different dimensions of this new phenomenon. Most people will have heard of the attempts on Fidel Castro's life by former agents collaborating with the CIA (or factions within it) and with Miami gangsters. Not so well known is the fact that spook Walt Mackem planned an invasion of the small island of Abaco, with the aim of establishing it as an independent entity separate from the Bahamas. It was spooks in the service of two murderous dictators who were responsible for the murders of former Chilean ambassador Letellier in Washington, and of a prominent Basque expert on the Dominican Republic (author of *The Era of Trujillo*). Spook Mitch Werbel organized background scenes of an invasion for a CBS movie – scenes that served as camouflage for a real invasion planned against Haiti, in order to set up a more effective centre of operations than Miami on the island, for use against the Cuban revolution. Colonel Allen Bell, boss of Dektor Counter-Intelligence Inc., has a long list of giant US corporations among his clients. The spooks of Fidelifacts tried to gather incriminating material to use against Ralph Nader on behalf of General Motors, and assumed the protection of IBM's data-bank.

Perhaps the most outrageous of all the business operations carried out by spooks was that mounted in the mid fifties by Robert Maheu, former right-hand of billionaire Howard Hughes, against the Greek shipping magnate Aristotle Onassis. Fabricating documents, manipulating US lawcourts, and using electronic eavesdropping devices on a lavish scale, Maheu tried to break Onassis, or at least sabotage the deal giving him a monopoly on oil transport from Saudi Arabia. Who was he acting for? The oil cartel? Some faction in the CIA? Competitors? All of these in collaboration? Probably we shall never know.

Such sensational activities could hardly fail to inspire a new sub-genre, the 'true' political thriller. Here the central theme is conspiracy, often with a generous spicing of 'revelations' offering inside dope on what really goes on behind the scenes in world politics. Especially since Watergate, the conspiracies portrayed often involve hypothetical presidents of the United States of America, whether thinly disguised real ones, or imaginary creations. But we also encounter reincarnations of the late Shah of Iran; Saudi Arabian politicians, oil sheikhs, and their Lebanese go-betweens; Israeli ministers, generals or Mossad chiefs; international terrorists; greedy Swiss bankers; German politicians with plans for a Fourth Reich; Italian tycoons plotting military coups, with or without Mafia assistance; innumerable agents of the KGB or the Chinese secret service; and so on.

Examples of the new genre include Frederick Forsyth's *The Odessa File* (1972), Robert Ludlum's *The Holcroft Covenant* (1978), Morris West's decidedly superior *Salamander* (1977), *Harlequin* (1974), and *Proteus* (1979), Robert Hawkey's *Side Effect* (1979), and Walter Stovall's *Presidential Emergency* (1978), in which a supposed US president actually defects to the People's Republic of China! Novels of this kind take on a particularly 'spooky' dimension when actually written by former high government officials or office-holders: instances that come to mind include former Vice-President Spiro T. Agnew's *The Canfield*

Decision (1976), and a thinly disguised *roman à clef, The Company* (1976) by John Ehrlichmann, previously Nixon's top aide in the White House.

15. From an integrative to a disintegrative function of the crime story

The crime story's ideological function is not simply an objective one, derived from the influence it exercises over the majority of its readers, or from the kind of ideas it helps to spread and the way in which these legitimize bourgeois society and its values. At least for a whole historical period, it has also been the result of a conscious choice of authors themselves.

It is revealing to study the biographies of some of the most famous classical detective writers. These show to what extent such figures as Sir Arthur Conan Doyle, Maurice Leblanc, Agatha Christie, Dorothy Sayers, or G. K. Chesterton were ultra-conservative upholders of the established order (not to speak of lesser writers like Edgar Wallace or E. Philip Oppenheim grotesquely ranting on about 'bolshevik conspirators' in 1920s Britain: Edgar Wallace, 'I hate the British worker').[1]

Such neo-classical authors as Dashiell Hammett, Georges Simenon, Claude Aveline and Rex Stout represented a typically transitional phenomenon. Hammett worked for eight years as a Pinkerton agent, deployed against strikers and left-wing organizations. From there he transferred to a private detective agency without any involvement in the class struggle. He then moved into writing for pulp magazines, and finally towards 'serious' detective novels. This evolution was a conscious one: Hammett felt bad about having helped employers fight striking workers, and deliberately chose to change his job. (He is said on one occasion to have rejected an offer from Anaconda Copper to kill the working class leader Frank Little.) He himself has written of this choice. He was subsequently to move further in the direction of a left-wing literary milieu, becoming the companion of Communist author

Lilian Hellman. This did not mean that the novels he wrote after this turn in his life explicitly opposed bourgeois values: they did nothing of the kind, as I attempted to show in an earlier chapter. But they did stop treating those who oppose law, order, property or decency, as self-evident criminals.

Rex Stout followed a rather different trajectory. He is said to have begun his literary career as an avowed radical, perhaps even a sympathizer of the Communist Party. Later he moved politically to the right, as shown by the clear concessions to McCarthyism in some of his novels. While not even his earliest works (some of which, like *Fer de Lance* or *Too Many Cooks*, are among his best) constitute any kind of break with bourgeois ideology, they do nevertheless present a rather more ambiguous picture of an upper-class milieu than do the stories of, for example, an Agatha Christie.

Georges Simenon, in a discussion with J. Altwegg (*Die Zeit*, 2 April 1976), stated categorically:

> Ninety per cent of the population … are slaves … including the higher and even the top-most grades of the employed, slaves who do not notice that they are exploited by a tiny minority. And this minority does not even represent the other ten per cent of the population. Even our politicians, whether they know it or not, are really and truly under the thumb of a few corporations that dominate everything and everybody.

Raymond Chandler is the exception in this group of writers. He got into big oil money during the boom of the twenties, but lost his fortune in the Depression. Then he achieved fame and wealth once again ten years later as a Hollywood writer. Although he described his hero Philip Marlowe as a rebel against a corrupt society, Chandler himself ended up by adapting to corruption: not just material, but also moral corruption, as a supporter of McCarthyism.

By contrast, Claude Aveline was a member of the French Communist Party (or at least a fellow-traveller) at the time that he wrote many of his mystery stories.

The turn, to which these novels represented a transition, was to appear most clearly, however, with the advent of the spy story. The very nature of the spy as an agent of state power (albeit a hostile, alien one) meant that service to the state, hence the nature of the state, hence the nature of law and order itself, ceased to be identified with absolute Good, against which Evil alone can raise its ugly head. The relative, ambiguous character of law and order now entered the mystery story on a massive scale. Some laws are good, some are bad; one order has to be upheld, another has to be fought against. This is no longer bourgeois ideology in its quintessential form.

The breach in the detective novel's integrative function with respect to bourgeois society was widened considerably with the explosion of (often blind) violence in the fifties; with the widespread use of informers by the police and the consequent growing interpenetration between police, informers and criminals; with the large-scale penetration of legitimate business by organized crime, and the former's increasing use of illegal or actually criminal methods; with the growing symbiosis between crime, big business and a reinforced state. As we have seen, these developments found their reflection in mystery stories and thrillers.

Of necessity, this reflection moved away from any Manichaean representation of society. While the criminal was not generally treated any more sympathetically than before, the established order itself gradually became more and more ambiguous, more and more closely identified with shady methods, corruption, compromises on basic values. What was initially true for hostile foreign states in the spy story now increasingly became true for the writer's own state too. Law and order ceased to be absolutely Good: they became relative, ambiguous, dubious. The individual fighter against crime – whether private eye or honest cop – ceased to be a self-confident, 'positive' hero from the bourgeois point of view. They became almost tragic figures, operating within the framework and in the service of an Establishment in which they believed less and less, which they even began to hate and despise.

The biography of Graham Greene offers a striking illustration of this evolution, as seen through his novels. Greene started out as a conservative agent of the British intelligence services, upholding such reactionary causes as the struggle of the Catholic Church against the Mexican revolution (*The Power and the Glory*, 1940), and arguing the necessary merciful function of religion in a context of human misery (*Brighton Rock*, 1938; *The Heart of the Matter*, 1948).

However, the better he came to know the socio-political realities of the third world where he was operating, and the more directly he came to be confronted by the rising tide of revolution in those countries, the more his doubts regarding the imperialist cause grew, and the more his novels shifted away from any identification with the latter. In *Our Man in Havana* (1958), he was still only poking fun at the imperialist spy establishment. But whereas Greene had been extremely hostile to the Malayan and Kenyan guerrilla fighters, his attitude began to change in Vietnam (*The Quiet American*, 1955) and, as he described in his autobiography (*Ways of Escape*, 1980), hardened still further in an anti-imperialist direction in Zaire (*A Burnt-Out Case*, 1961), Haiti (*The Comedians*, 1964), Paraguay (*The Honorary Consul*, 1973), and South Africa (*The Human Factor*, 1978). This evolution culminated in his eloquent denunciation of the real-life interpenetration between gangsterism and the public authorities (including the judiciary) in the Nice region of southern France, in his latest book *J'Accuse* — banned in France by the 'socialist' government of Mitterrand and Mauroy.

The altered ideological content of the mystery and spy story, and the new tragic role of the hero, are best illustrated by a whole series of books that appeared in the sixties: most notably *The Spy Who Came in from the Cold* (1963) and subsequent novels by John Le Carré, and Len Deighton's *The Billion Dollar Brain*. Now 'our' Establishment is portrayed as being (almost) as bad as 'theirs'. Worse still, as the hero fights the Enemy, the hero is not only fully aware of defending a dubious cause, but also expects to be regularly betrayed and stabbed in the back by the masters. Very gradually, the hero slips once again into the role of a rebel, rather than a supporter of law and order. Other top thrillers of recent years that illustrate the same trend include *Gorky Park* (1981) and *Marathon Man* (1974). In the latter, the distinction between 'good' spies (ours) and 'bad' ones (theirs) is virtually non-existent: the operators have become anonymous agents of unknown nationality, selling their services indifferently to a succession of powers (and former powers, in the shape of a top Nazi war criminal). All are, incidentally, supreme experts in the noble art of murder. The real hero of the book is no longer someone chasing a criminal, but an innocent boy fighting for his life against agents conspiring in the name of heaven knows what. By an internal logic of its own, the thriller has here come very close to Kafka's universe, with the innocent as K. The dividing line between crime and established order, evil and punishment, has vanished.

This evolution of the crime story, of course, means that it can no longer function as a literary genre helping to persuade its readers to accept the legitimacy of bourgeois society. Its integrative function has declined, and it has actually become disintegrative with respect to that society. Objectively, it has begun to contribute to a questioning by millions of people of basic bourgeois values. However, it is one thing to question or objectively undermine bourgeois ideology, quite another to reject it consciously and across the board. This becomes possible only if another set of ideas and values can be counterposed to it. Nothing of the kind has occurred, even in the most sophisticated variants of the contemporary thriller.[2]

In the first place, the fundamental structure of the mystery story remains one in which an individual hero opposes a great criminal, a personification of evil, or some anonymous machine. This confrontation based upon an individual is congruent with the bourgeois order: it is simply the ultimate rationalization of the competition between private commodity-owners on the market-place.

In the second place, individual revolt against the prevalent corrupt and corrupting bourgeois values (let alone individual revolt against the existing bourgeois order) is in the long run ineffective and doomed to failure. It is a labour of Sisyphus: eliminate one crooked cop and ten will appear; suppress one unscrupulous real-estate speculator and a dozen new ones will pop up immediately; cut one tyrannical tycoon down to size and five corporations will at once fuse and give birth to a yet more tyrannical monopolist. Individual revolt inevitably leads into a blind alley: 'You can't fight City Hall.' Only collective, organized revolt, rooted in social forces with an objective potential and subjective will to transcend bourgeois society – rooted in the working class – offers any way out. But such collective revolt rarely has anything to do with the content of thrillers.

This is why, even in the best cases, the sophisticated thriller's hero has to be a tragic figure, a petty-bourgeois (in no pejorative sense) rather than a proletarian-revolutionary protagonist. This is why the farthest the sophisticated thriller can go on the ideological level is to reveal and intensify the general crisis of bourgeois ideology that characterizes late capitalism. It cannot reach the point of breaking totally with that ideology or transcending it.

This basic contradiction, affecting even the most progressive end-results of the mystery story's evolution, is clearly illustrated by two precursors of the socially critical school, Le Breton and Friedrich Dürrenmatt. (Some critics put G. K. Chesterton in the same category, but I cannot agree: although Chesterton's Father Brown does not like rich people or approve of capital accumulation, he has a dogmatic conception of Good and Evil that is entirely consistent with upholding the stability of bourgeois society. The case of Le Breton and Dürrenmatt is quite different.)

Le Breton, often called the anarchist among crime writers, deliberately constructs his plots not around any conflict between criminals on the one hand and official or amateur enforcers of the law on the other, but around conflicts among criminals themselves. 'Good' criminals, individualistic rebels against a rotten and corrupt society, respect certain rules, do not collaborate with cops, follow a code of honour, do not betray their accomplices, divide the spoils fairly within the gang. 'Bad' criminals double-cross each other freely, steal each other's companions, kill each other to increase their own share of the loot, do not hesitate to sell out to the cops in order to save their own skin, use the lowest form of blackmail to eliminate competition, force their attentions on women. In this sombre, desperate universe, individual honour appears as the only index of integrity. The petty-bourgeois, or pre-bourgeois, nature of that anarchist revolt against bourgeois society is manifest.

The same conclusion may be drawn from Dürrenmatt's classic detective novels *The Judge and his Hangman* (1950) and *Suspicion*

(1951). Police Commissioner Bärlach has seen through the hypocrisy and corruption of bourgeois society:

> Bourgeois order is no longer just. I know how it works ... the big crooks are left free, only the small fry are captured ... a nice businessman often commits a crime between his Martini and his lunch, simply by hatching some sharp business deal: a crime that nobody suspects of being one, least of all the businessman himself. (p. 136)

But Bärlach reacts against this unjust social order in a purely individualistic way. One might even say that the police chief becomes an anarchist militant before his death. He does not actually throw bombs, but he sets traps for bourgeois criminals and has them killed by third parties. By acting in this way, Bärlach sets himself up as a judge of Good and Evil, outside – and sometimes against – the Law. He and he alone decides who deserves to be killed, and how it will be done. By giving a police chief this function and presenting him as a socially critical, even anti-bourgeois hero, Dürrenmatt certainly gives an audacious and paradoxical new twist to the crime story. But the innovation remains within the framework of the moral contrast between good and evil; the framework of individual competition between hero and villain (even though the latter in the case will be an honoured pillar of society). The frontiers of bourgeois ideology ultimately remain inviolate, and the same vulgar ideological assumptions are purveyed as those encapsulated by Simenon in the formula: 'Man does not change.'

One might be forgiven for expecting that the series of crime novels by Manuel Vazquez Montalban, himself a member of the Central Committee of the Catalan Communist Party, would prove an exception to the norm I have been describing. Unfortunately, they are nothing of the kind. *Murder in the Central Committee* (in English, 1984), for example, remains a classic confrontation between good and evil individuals, albeit submerged in a hazy atmosphere of ambiguity. The murderer is a CIA agent, recruited thanks to a vulgar and urgent need for money. The detective hero is a former communist and also a former CIA agent, politically sceptical, intent on purely private, erotic and gastronomic adventures. In other words, the novel's world view is a typically petty-bourgeois one, with perhaps a pinch of Stalinist salt in the ubiquity of 'agents'. In general all Montalban's books are soaked in an atmosphere of spleen, scepticism and *fin-de-siècle* ennui, very significant as the background of a whole layer of intellectual Eurocommunists. It is a break with Stalinist dogmatism and hypocrisy, but hardly a step towards greater lucidity of what this society and this world are all about.

In this context, some mention should perhaps be made of a book that pitches Sherlock Holmes against a potential murderer of Karl Marx in London: *Marx et Sherlock Holmes* (1980), by Alexis Lecage. At the margins of outright parody, however, this work really forms part of a growing series of attempts to extend the Master Detective's exploits beyond his creator's death. (Another example is Michael Hardwick's *Prisoner of the Devil* (1981), in which Holmes's client is Alfred Dreyfus on Devil's Island!) A more serious candidate for consideration as a work opposed to bourgeois ideology is Chris Mullin's *A Very British Coup* (1982), in which the editor of *Tribune* portrays a left-wing Labour government being overthrown in 1989 by a conspiracy involving big business and organized crime.

The best, but also in a sense the most tragic, example of a 'disintegrative' crime story is Sam Greenlee's *The Spook Who Sat by the Door* (1969). (The echo of Le Carré in the title is, of course, not accidental.) Greenlee recounts the saga of a black nationalist in the United States who, after infiltrating the CIA and the 'social workers' racket, builds up a network of young street gangs with the aim of smashing the white power structure by waging urban guerrilla warfare in the Northern cities.

The book is evidently a product of the black ghetto revolts in the mid sixties. However, the author failed to understand what subsequent experience has shown. Street gangs of the kind he describes cannot either trigger off mass revolts of the black proletariat and sub-proletariat, or relate to the exploited working-class majority of the white population, because they have an essentially substitutionist outlook. In the best of cases, they do indeed want to capture the sympathy of the masses; but they do not help these masses to organize themselves for self-emancipation – something which is dismissed as utopian. In reality, however, the notion of confronting the most powerful repressive apparatus on the globe with a small, dedicated minority lacking any mass organization is itself blatantly utopian – indeed it is clearly suicidal.

The really tragic thing about this book is that Greenlee shows himself more aware than any other thriller writer not just of how the white establishment treats the black and latino population in the United States, but of the oppressive, exploitative and inhuman nature of bourgeois society in general. He is filled with legitimate scorn for all the liberals and reformists (whether black or white) who are ready to accept oppression and exploitation, in exchange for a few token concessions.

But his own alternative to alienation is itself alienated and alienating: secret elite organization for destructive purposes only; rejection of any mass organization or self-help; lack of understanding of the fundamental truth that the educators themselves need to be educated: that there exists no elite possessing the whole truth from the outset; that only a constant dialectical interplay between vanguard organization and mass spontaneity is truly emancipatory in that it can lead to a *self*-emancipation of the masses. Thus, even through its best product, the socially conscious thriller strikingly confirms the inherent limitations of the genre. Because it still respects the basic ground rules of the genre – the individual confrontation between hero and villain, in this case an individual hero facing a collective villain – it can attain only partial social consciousness.

16. Closing the circle?

In *The Road to Gandolfo* (1976), Robert Ludlum breaks the golden rule: crime *does* pay. And what a crime: nothing less than the kidnapping of a (consenting) pope, funded by a Mafia boss, a British tycoon, and an Arab comprador sheikh! In this novel, the borderline between legality and illegality, high society and the underworld, the state apparatus and organized crime, diplomacy and treachery, has entirely disappeared. The hero is an American army general who exclaims at one point:

> Goddam, boy, I've spent thirty-some years in this man's army. You take off the uniform … I'm as naked as a plucked duck. I only *know* the army; I don't know anything else, I'm not trained for anything if you come right down to it … The only goddamned thing I'm trained for is to be a crook, maybe … And I'd probably fuck that up because I don't give that much of a damn about money.

It would be hard to summarize better the growing symbiosis between state and crime, under the stimulus of big money! Has the wheel now turned full circle? Has the systematic recourse by monopolists to illegal methods, the corruption of themselves and the state apparatus that defends their interests, reached a point where the universe of the crime story has been turned upside down and the criminal has once again, as at its origins, become an object of sympathy?

The trend would certainly seem to be in this direction. Even the late John Creasey, in his *Gideon's Law* (1971), portrays police accused of unlawful brutality as poor victims of persecution, saved in the nick of time from final disgrace by the righteousness of their commander and the tricks of their officers. There has been an undeniable tendency in recent years to justify not merely crime, but outright murder – even mass murder. In Adam Hall's *The Damocles Sword* (1981), the hero is an upper-class British spy who infiltrates the Nazi machine in the guise of an SS colonel, in order to bring out of the Third Reich some scientists capable of working on the atomic bomb. In the course of his mission, he kills twenty-eight men with his bare hands, driven more by homicidal rage than by professional duty. It is true that some of his victims are heinous and sadistic criminals themselves; but others are minor figures like taxi-drivers or ordinary police. Nevertheless, this mass murderer is portrayed as just as much of a knight in shining armour at the end of the horrible story as he was at the outset, before becoming a maniacal killer.

Eric Van Lustbader's *The Ninja* (1979) is another recent bestselling thriller, well researched, well written, and full of suspense, whose central hero is a murderer. This time he murders to protect an unscrupulous, murderous American tycoon against an attempt on his life by an equally murderous Japanese tycoon (or is it really to take his revenge because the Japanese tycoon stole his girl?). All the author's sympathies are clearly with the murderer. Although one of the police is presented sympathetically as well, others are decidedly not. Moreover, the author closes the story with a broad hint that the murderer will now kill the American tycoon too – with his full approval.

In *The Evil That Men Do* (1978), Lance Hill depicts, to quote the book's cover:

> an international assassin [Holland] whose lethal skills are for sale if the price and the cause are right. He must penetrate the Doctor's defences and nail his quarry with a single, well-aimed bullet. The Doctor [is] the most demonic master of torture since the Nazis, who taught the Chilean generals, the Greek colonels, and the Shah's SAVAK the savage refinements of his art. Now he lives deep in the Guatemalan jungle, shielded by the CIA.

To think it possible to fight torture by killing a single torturer is pure utopia. And to do it for money is not very nice, to say the least. So whatever sympathies we may have for Holland's political preferences, and however much we may hate the Doctor's trade and the regimes he serves, Holland still remains a murderer. This turning of murderer into hero marks a significant return to the treatment of 'good rebels' in the picaresque novel from which the detective story originally sprang.

To take a further example, in *Shibumi* (1980) author Trevanian presents as the hero one Nicholai Hel, who opposes the Mother Company, 'a consortium of major international petroleum, communications and transportation corporations' that also controls the CIA and the executive branch of the US government, and is in cahoots with Arab oil sheikhs and the PLO. The Mother Company's power derives in part from its super-computer (inevitably!) that contains so much data that 'asking the right questions in the right form' of it has become a real and most difficult art. Hel hates 'merchants' and American bomber planes, after traumatic experiences in Shanghai in 1937 and in wartime Japan, where he was tutored by a Japanese general and a Gō teacher. He is, in the author's words, 'the most deadly assassin in the world', who has killed countless people, either for money or in the service of 'idealistic' counter-terrorism. Yet he is certainly the novel's real hero. Incidentally, in the same work the British Secret Service, in the course of a routine diversionary operation designed to cover its tracks vis-à-vis its Arab masters (*sic*), kills one hundred and fifty of its own agents!

Ludlum, Van Lustbader, Hill and Trevanian are by no means exceptions; many other names could be added to the list. In Stephen King's *The Dead Zone* (1979), a fine book on the border between the thriller and 'real' literature, the main character Johnny Smith attempts to murder a nasty demagogue out to capture the US presidency and capable of unleashing world war three. So sympathetic do the hero and his cause appear that the reader can only regret that the planned murder fails in the end. Again, in Robert Rosenblum's *The Good Thief* a private detective, to avenge his girl-friend's death from an overdose, kills two unarmed dope-pushers.   Similar instances of personal revenge as motive for a war against crime have figured in innumerable novels, comic strips, films and television series in recent years. The whole development was foreshadowed in Peter O'Donnell's Modesty Blaise series, which began to appear in the sixties. Blaise is a war refugee who, following an odyssey through Eastern Europe and the Middle East, succeeds in building up a network of thieves and smugglers in Tangiers. She and her friend Willie Garvin, having grown immensely rich through 'selective crime' (murder excluded), take up good causes just as the 'good bandits' of yore did. As 'poachers turned gamekeepers', they defend the innocent, the poor and the threatened against 'bad' gangsters of every kind.

The explanation for this return of the crime story to the primordial pattern of the outlaw hero lies, above all, in the very climate that I have described of growing scepticism about law and order, and the state. More and more of the public that reads thrillers or detective stories have a cynical attitude towards the police and law enforcement. Police methods are seen as in no way morally superior to those used by criminals. Society is seen as being rotten through and through. Crime writers thus have to adapt to this general mood. If Simenon, Dürrenmatt, Greene, Le Carré already did so in their various ways, the writers I have just been discussing went all the way. Their heroes are no longer disabused spies or police: they are now criminals once more.

There is nothing astonishing about the fact that decaying capitalism, expressed as it is in a decay of bourgeois values, should give rise to formal patterns in the relationship between criminals and the law similar to those that characterized rising capitalism two centuries earlier. However, the similarity is, precisely, just a formal one. For the 'noble bandits' of the picaresque novels that gave birth to the detective story were rebels with a cause. Like the revolutionary bourgeois, they not only knew what to fight against – injustice, torture, intolerance, oppression, absolutist power, judicial corruption, etc. – but were also quite aware of what they were fighting for : personal freedom and formal equality of rights; justice based on a written code of law; generosity and sympathy towards the oppressed and the poor in general.

The noble bandits of our own day, however, are rebels without a cause, disillusioned and cynical. Even when they know what they are fighting against – SS torturers, for example, reactionary tycoons, pathological killers, or dope-pushers and their bosses – they have no idea what they are fighting for, or worse still know that they are fighting for nothing. They no longer believe in anything, except perhaps the possibility of finding some small niche of personal happiness in the short term. Their rebellion stems not from hope but from bitterness; not from love for the oppressed but from hatred of oppression; from a rejection of society as it is, but not from any notion that it might be possible to replace it by a better one.

Yesterday's noble bandit was the petty-bourgeois forerunner of the coming bourgeois revolution. Today's is the petty-bourgeois rebel against a decaying bourgeois present, and individual sensitivity or even heroism cannot hide the social impotence of their class. They are rebels without a cause because their class has no social perspective opposed to that of bourgeois society; because it has no independent future. They are certainly no forerunners of socialist revolution.

Thus the balance sheet of this new revolt, this striking return to the criminal-as-hero, is ambiguous to say the least. It is, of course, true that the rejection of prevailing social values in the latest phase of the crime novel is a destabilizing rather than a stabilizing factor for bourgeois society. At the same time, however, the idealization of private vengeance, of private violence directed against criminals, is extremely ominous. For these products of imagination correspond to a terrifying spread in real life of vigilante or 'self-defence' violence. They thus help to foster and justify such violence, which in turn increasingly takes on a pre-fascist or proto-fascist content, with a clearly xenophobic and racist central thrust – leading to pogrom-like assaults on North African communities in France, Asian or West Indian ones in Britain, Turkish ones in Germany, black or hispanic ones in the United States, etc. Hence, by a striking ideological twist, we find that whereas the 'good bandit' of earlier centuries with few exceptions fought for equality and against discrimination or intolerance, the counterpart in the late twentieth century typically fights for inequality and is ethnically or racially discriminatory.

Furthermore, the downgrading of law and order in the

contemporary thriller, though in itself not objectionable in principle, may have effects that go far beyond the mere reappearance of the good bandit as hero. Every form of crime, even what is most degrading to human dignity, may be rendered banal, or brave. This underlines a point I made earlier: that the decay of bourgeois values does not automatically have positive results. It may indeed go together with the emergence of higher social values. But it may equally move towards a general decline of all human values, any kind of humanism, any recognition of the basic sanctity of human life and the basic dignity of all human beings.

The spread of video games and the fierce competition this has unleashed has led to a frenetic search for special needs to serve, in order to expand each manufacturer's share of the market. In one recent game, 'Streetlife', the player has to assume the role of a pimp. His life is not an easy one, his worries are many. Should he invest in a Chrysler Baron or a Cadillac Eldorado? How much should he pay his prostitutes, their bodyguards, his lawyers, and the cops? In the words of the game's inventor, Arthur Wood (a television reporter at a local station in Houston, Texas): 'The players immerse themselves completely in this pitiful universe and can solve the problem only by adopting the values [sic] of the most ignoble of pimps.' Apparently Wood sees no moral problem in making money by disseminating this ignoble pimp's values: once again, *non olet*. His next creation seemingly involves the simulation of different sexual acts by a computer! (For all this, see *Libération*, 2 September 1982.)

Thus the evolution of the crime story does indeed reflect, as if in a mirror, the evolution of bourgeois ideology, of social relations in bourgeois society, perhaps even of the capitalist mode of production itself. Remarkably, a German conservative ideologue, Johannes Gross, has noted the same correspondence between the detective story and bourgeois society, and has attempted to situate it historically:

> In feudal times no detective story could have been written, if only because it requires a rational system of law... The detective of the classical crime novel is an expression of a society that is capable of ordering its own business, free from

outside interference; in none of the books now regarded as classics does the detective belong to a social group different from that in which the crime takes place – in other words, the highest layers of society…Today the rule of bourgeois order is finished [A rather premature judgement, alas! E.M.], finished like the great ideologies of the nineteenth century… And every news report about the disintegration or abandonment of bourgeois institutions is simultaneously a postscript to the crime novel.' (See 'Nachwort zum Kriminalroman', in *Lauter Nachworte: Innenpolitik nach Adenauer*)

The history of the crime story is a social history, for it appears intertwined with the history of bourgeois society itself. If the question is asked why it should be reflected in the history of a specific literary genre, the answer is: because the history of bourgeois society is also that of property and of the negation of property, in other words, crime; because the history of bourgeois society is also the growing, explosive contradiction between individual needs or passions and mechanically imposed patterns of social conformism; because bourgeois society in and of itself breeds crime, originates in crime, and leads to crime; perhaps because bourgeois society is, when all is said and done, a criminal society?

Notes

1. From hero to villain

1. Shi Nai'an and Luo Guanzhong, *Outlaws of the Marsh*, Indiana University Press, Bloomington, Ind. 1981. Robert van Gulik (*Willow Pattern*, 1965), a Dutch diplomat who became a writer of detective stories, created a fictional seventh-century Chinese judge, Jen-Dieh Dee, whom some critics have mistakenly considered to be a historical figure. He is, of course, a fictional character, although van Gulik's stories are based on real judicial records. There can be no talk, however, of 'classical' Chinese detective stories, for the tradition van Gulik recounts has to do with the effort to oppose the arbitrary rule of mandarins or other oppressors more than with solving mysteries.

2. Today's unreflected popular literature (*Trivialliteratur*) has two components: the crime story (and its precursor, the Western) and 'romantic women's literature'. Press runs are similar in the two genres: compare the figures quoted on pp. 78-9 with the numbers of copies sold by the 'queen' and 'king' of romantic literature (Barbara Cartland: 100 million; Harold Robbins: 200 million). One German author, Johannes Mario Simmel, has crossed from one genre to the other, selling a total of 55 million copies of his works, a remarkable figure for a writer in the German language. But then, he is a remarkable person, whose latest crime story, *Bitte lasst die Blumen leben* (*Please Let the Flowers Live*, 1982), has also crossed the threshold of serious literature, and contains a progressive political message too.

3. According to Löwy (*Die Weltgeschichte ist das Weltgericht*), Bukharin was a fanatical reader of detective stories, who arrived

late at important party meetings because he couldn't drag himself away from a thriller he was currently reading.

2. From villain to hero

1. Several of Dickens's other books are crime stories of a kind, among them *Barnaby Rudge* and, of course, the unfinished *Mystery of Edwin Drood*.
2. See the interesting discussion of the 'reverse story', or 'backward construction and the art of suspense', in Dennis Porter, *The Pursuit of Crime*, Yale University Press, 1981, pp.24 ff.

3. From the streets to the drawing room

1. Monsignor Ronald A. Knox, the English essayist and religious apologist, wrote several detective stories as well as 'Ten Commandments of Detection' (Introduction to *The Best Detective Stories*, London 1929). There he actually states: 'No Chinaman must figure in the story...'

5. The ideology of the detective story

1. Our Swiss friend Marc Perrenoud has worked out the first attempt at a Marxist analysis of humanity's relation with death (Marx: *la Mort et les Autres*, mimeographed manuscript). For two recent books about the social history of death see Michel Vovelle, *La Mort et l'Occident de 1300 à nos jours* (Paris 1983) and Philippe Ariès, *L'Homme devant la Mort* (Paris 1977).
2. The Japanese detective story originated with Edogawa Rampo in the 1920s (*Nisen Doka*, 'The Two-Sen Copper Coin', 1923), but really developed after world war two: 14 million copies of crime stories were sold in the mid-sixties, 20 million in the mid-seventies. Apart from Rampo, the main authors are Seicho Matsumoto, Masahi Yokomizo (*The Honjin Murder Case*, 1947), Yoh Sano, and Shizuko Natsuki (*The Passed Death*). All these references come from Ellery Queen, *Japanese Golden*

> *Dozen: The Detective Story World in Japan,* Charles E. Tuttle, Tokyo 1972.

3. On this psychopathology of violence, note this passage from Jack Higgins's thriller *Solo* (Pan, London 1980-1):

> 'Rules of the game. They weren't the target.'
>
> 'The game?' Morgan said. 'And what game would that be?'
>
> 'You should know. You have been playing it long enough. The most exciting game in the world, with your own life as the ultimate stake. Can you honestly tell me anything else you've done that offered quite the same kick?'
>
> 'You're mad,' Morgan said.
>
> Mikali looked fairly surprised. 'Why? I used to do the same things in uniform and they gave me medals for it. Your own position exactly. When you look in the mirror it's me you see.'

> Mikali is a famous concert soloist and a psychopathological killer. Morgan is a highly placed army officer and something of a psychopathological killer too.

7. From organized crime to state crime

1. Two Soviet emigrant authors, Edward Topol and Fredrikh Neznausky, wrote a book in a similar vein, *Red Square,* (London 1983), full of information about the Soviet establishment. Neznausky had been a criminal lawyer in the USSR for 25 years.

2. 'Violence is not the primary end of organized crime, but a means to the goal of profit maximization.' 'Organized crime is a social institution. Whether it is good or bad or both is a matter of moral judgement. But ethics apart, it is in the same general category as religion, politics, business, unionism, the military, and education. It comes into being the same way as these other institutions as the natural expression of a group of people engaged in a common purpose.' The author of that remarkable

observation is Gus Tyler, a leading American trade unionist. The quotations are taken from Francis A. J. Ianni and Elizabeth Reuss-Ianni, *The Crime Society: Organized Crime and Corruption in America*, New American Library, New York 1976, pp. 273 and 119.

8. Mass production and mass consumption

1. Interestingly enough, the small fry engaged in state snooping – e.g. the British GCHQ at Cheltenham, seem to feel these frustrations in a particularly sharp way because of the ambiguity of their labour. The *Sunday Times* (15 April 1984) reported that George Franks, the GCHQ radio officer found dead at his Sussex home, was the fourth man in two years to die suddenly. The deaths raise an important question: are British eavesdroppers working under too much stress?

9. Outward diversification

1. Like Conan Doyle, Dorothy Sayers and other popularly successful authors, Karl May lived his hoped-for life in his books. He was a notorious liar, he conned people, and he didn't know any foreign languages, including English, his summary use of English words in his Wild West novels notwithstanding. See his biography by Erich Loest, *Swallon, Mein Schwarzer Mustang?*, Fischer-Taschenbuch 1982.
2. This is, of course, no accident. Without going into the deeper ideological reasons for the phenomenon, one can understand the material basis of this absence. Detecting takes time. Detectives, therefore, are either paid professionals or genteel people of 'independent means'. Wage-workers are neither one nor the other. They have no time of their own for detecting. Their time belongs to their bosses. The boss prefers them to produce surplus value rather than discovering whodunit.
3. As the manuscript of this book was being finished, the exciting news arrived that Isaac Asimov, the science fiction writer, has located a crime story in which a robot is being 'killed' in outer space.

4. Edmund Wilson goes wrong, though, on Rex Stout's *The Red Box*. He did not read through the whole book and so never learned that there really were two red boxes, one, as he says, a hoax, but the second and genuine one actually containing the evidence to confound the murderer.

12. From crime to business

1. On the origins of the Bronfman family fortune, see Peter C. Newman, *Bronfman Dynasty*, Toronto: Seal Books 1978.

14. State, business and crime

1. See Rupert Cornwall, *God's Banker*, London: Gollancz 1983. More controversial is Richard Hammer's *The Vatican Connection*, 1982.
2. In Cuba, a book was recently published dealing sympathetically with the crime story. A member of the Central Committee of the Bulgarian Communist Party, Bogomil Rainov, is the author of detective stories that enjoy a wide circulation in Eastern Europe.

15. From an integrative to disintegrative function of the crime story

1. The identical formulae is used by the upper-class novelist Vita Sackville-West.
2. The most successful post-war German crime story writer, Friedrick Werremeier, is not shy to point out the commercial interest of keeping social criticism within certain bonds: 'Students recently asked me how much social criticism a crime story of normal length could get away with. I answered hesitantly, 'Around 40%'. (Hans-Jürgen Bartelheimer's manuscript, p. 44.)

Bibliography

Philippe Ariès, *L'Homme devant la Mort*, Paris, 1977.

John Ball, *The Mystery Story*, San Diego, 1976.

Earl F. Bargainnier, *The Gentle Art of Murder*, Bowling Green, 1980.

Jacques Barzun, *The Delights of Detection*, New York, 1961.

Jacques Barzun and Wendell Hartig, *A Catalogue of Crime*, New York, 1971.

Walter Benjamin, 'Kriminalromane auf Reisen', in *Gesammelte Werke*, Vol. 10.

Stefano Benvenuti and Gianni Rizzioni, *An Informal History of Detective Fiction*, New York, 1980.

Ernest Bloch, 'Philosophische Ansicht des Detektivromans' in *Literarische Aufsätze, Gesammelte Werke* Vol. 19, Frankfurt, 1965.

Anton Blok, On Brigandage with special reference to peasant mobilization, in *Sociologische Gids*, 1971.

Hans Blumenherz, *Die Lesbarkeit der Welt*, Frankfurt, 1981.

Boileau and Narcejac, *Le Roman Policier*, Paris, 1975.

James Brabazon, *Dorothy Sayers: The Life of a Courageous Woman*, London, 1981.

Bertolt Brecht, 'Ueber die Popularität des Detektivromans', in *Gasammelte Werke* Vol. 16, Berlin, 1976.

Frank Browning and John Gerassi, *The American Way of Crime*, New York, 1980.

Peter Brückner, *Sigmund Freud's Privatlektüre*, Köln, 1975.

John Carter, 'Collecting Detective Fiction', in Howard Haycraft, *The Life and Times of the Detective Story*, New York, 1941.

John G. Cawelti, *Adventure, Mystery and Romance*, Chicago, 1976.

Raymond Chandler, 'The Simple Art of Murder', in *Atlantic Monthly*, December, 1944.

Raymond Chandler, *The Notebooks of Raymond Chandler* (ed. Frank McShane), London, 1977.

142 / Delightful Murder

Jean-Michel Charlier and Jean Marcilly, *Le Syndicat du Crime*, Paris, 1980.

Jean-Claude Chesnais, *Histoire de la Violence*, Paris, 1981.

Louis Chevalier, *Classes Laborieuses et Classes Dangereuses*, 2nd edition, Paris, 1978.

Agatha Christie, *An Autobiography*, London, 1977.

Javier Coma, *La Novela Negra*, Barcelona, 1980.

Rupert Cornwall, *God's Banker*, London, 1983.

Florian Coulmas, *Ueber Schrift*, Frankfurt, 1982.

David Craig (ed.), *Marxists on Literature*, Harmondsworth, 1975.

Alberto del Monte, *Breve Storia del Romanzo Poliziesco*, Milan, 1960.

Friedrich Depken, *Ein Beitrag zur Entwicklungsgeschichte und Technik der Kriminalerzählung*, Heidelberg, 1914.

P. H. de Vries, *Poe and After: The Detective-story Investigated*, Amsterdam, 1956.

César E. Diaz, *La Novela Policiaca*, Barcelona, 1973.

Raymond Dirks and Leonard Gross, *The Great Wall Street Scandal*, New York, 1974.

Dove, *The Police Procedural*, Bowling Green, 1982.

Arthur Conan Doyle, *Memories and Adventures*, London, 1924.

S. Dresden and S. Vestdijk, *Marionettenspel met de Dood*, The Hague, 1957.

E. du Perron, *Het Sprookje van de Misdaad*, Amsterdam, 1940.

Josée Dupuy, *Le Roman Policier*, Paris, 1974.

O. Eckert, *Der Kriminalroman als Gattung*, 1951.

Umberto Eco, 'Le Strutture Narrative in Fleming', in *L'Analisi del Racconto*, Milan, 1969.

Umberto Eco, *Postille a 'In nome della rosa'*, Milan, 1983.

Gerd Egloff, 'Mordrätsel oder Widerspiegelung der Gesellschaft?', in Erhard Schütz, *Zur Actualität des Kriminalromans*, Munich, 1978.

Friedrich Engels, 'Introduction' to Marx's 'The Civil War in France', in Marx and Engels, *Selected Works in Two Volumes*, Moscow, 1962.

E. Fischer, *The Necessity of Art*, Harmondsworth, 1959 (reprinted 1978).

F. Fosca, *Histoire et Technique du Roman Policier*, Paris, 1937.

Erich Fromm, *The Sane Society*, London, 1956.

Pierre Gascar, *Le Boulevard du Crime*, Paris, 1980.

Clifford Geertz, *The Interpretation of Cultures*, London, 1973.

W. Gerteis, *Detektive, ihre Geschichte im Leben und in der Literatur*, 1953.

Walter Gibson, *Touch, Sweet and Stuffy*, Bloomington, 1976.

Frères Goncourt, *Journal*, London, 1962.

Antonio Gramsci, 'Sul Romanzo poliziesco', in *Quaderni del Carcare*, Vol. V, Milan, 1964.

Robert Graves and Alan Hodge, *The Long Week-End*, London, 1940.

Graham Greene, *A Sort of Life*, New York, 1971.

Graham Greens, *Ways of Escape*, Harmondsworth, 1981.

David S. Gross in Roy R, Male (ed.), *Money Talks: Language and Lucre in American Fiction*, Oklahoma City, 1981.

Johannes Gross, *Lauter Nachworte, Innenpolitik nach Adenauer*, Stuttgart, 1965.

Roman Gubern, with A. Gramsci, Sergei Eisenstein et al., *La Novela Criminal*, Barcelona, 1970.

A.P. Hackett and J.H. Burke, *80 Years of Best-Sellers*, New York, 1977.

A. Ordean Hagen, *Who Done It?*, New York, 1969.

Peter Hairing, *Mystery! An Illustrated History of Crime and Detective Fiction*, London, 1973.

Richard Hammer, *The Vatican Connection*, 1982.

Ralph Harper, *The World of the Thriller*, Cleveland, 1969.

Howard Haycraft, *Murder for Pleasure*, New York, 1941.

Howard Haycraft, *The Art of the Mystery Story*, New York, 1946.

Howard Haycraft, *The Life and Times of the Detective Story*, New York, 1941.

G.W.F. Hegel, *Werke*, Vol. 13, *Verlesungen über Aesthetik*.

Rüdiger Herren, *Freud und die Kriminologie*, 1973.

Chester Himes, *The Quality of Hurt*, New York, 1972.

Chester Himes, *My Life of Absurdity*, New York, 1976.

Eric Hobsbawm, *Bandits*, London, 1969.

Eric Hobsbawm, *Primitive Rebels*, London, 1959.

Richard Hoggart, *The Uses of Literacy*, London, 1957.

Harold Horwood, *Newfoundland*, Toronto, 1969.

Mary Hottinger (Hrsgb.), *Wahre Morde*, Zurich, 1976.

Jim Hougan, *Spooks*, 1978.

F. Hoveyda, *Histoire du Roman Policier*, Paris, 1965.

Francis A.J. Ianni and Elizabeth Rauss Ianni (eds.), *The Crime Society*, New York, 1976.

Klaus Inderthal, 'Zur Geschichte und Theorie einer Populären Prosa: Detektiv- und Kriminal-Literatur', in Erhard Schütz, *Zur Aktualität des Kriminalromans*, Munich, 1978.

Neil H. Jacoby, Peter Nehemkis and Richard Eels, *Bribery and Extortion in World Business*, New York, 1977.

H. R. F. Keating (ed.), *Agatha Christie: First Lady of Crime*, London, 1977.

144 / Delightful Murder

H. R. F. Keating (ed.), *Sherlock Holmes: The Man and his World*, London, 1979.

G. Th. Kempe, *Over schrijvers, speurders, schurken*, Utrecht, 1947.

Stephen Knight, *Form and Ideology in Crime Fiction*, Bloomington, 1980.

Leo Kofler, *Soziologie des Ideologischen*, Stuttgart, 1975.

Siegfried Kracauer, *Le Roman Policier*, Paris, 1971.

Francis Lacassin, *Mythologie du Roman Policier*, Vol. 2, Paris, 1974.

Alain Lacombe, *Le Roman Noir Americain*, Paris, 1975.

Gavin Lambert, *The Dangerous Edge*, London, 1975.

Erik Lankester, *Zuidamerikaanse Misdaadverhalen*, Amsterdam, 1982.

Michael Laver, *The Crime Game*, Oxford, 1982.

Richard Layman, *The Shadow Man: The Life of Dashiell Hammett*, New York, 1980.

Erich Loest, *Swallon, mein schwarzer Mustang?*, Frankfurt, 1982.

A.G. Löwy, *Die Weltgeschichte ist das Weltgericht*, Vienna, 1969.

Ross MacDonald, *On Crime Writing*, Santa Barbara, 1973.

C.A. Madison, *Irving to Irving*, New York, 1974.

Karl Marx, 'Die Heilige Familie' Chapter 8, Marx and Engels, *Selected Works*, Vol. 2, Berlin, 1970.

Karl Marx, *Theories of Surplus Value*, Part I, Moscow, 1963.

Igor B. Maslowski, 'Une petite histoire du roman noir' (prologue to Leo Mallet's *A L'ombre du Grand Mur*, Paris, 1950).

Franz Mehring, 'Charles Dickens', in *Gesammelte Schriften*, Vol. 12, Berlin, 1976.

Regis Messac, *Le Detective Novel et l'Influence de la Pensée Scientifique*, Paris, 1929.

Steven F. Milliker, *Chester Himes: A Critical Appraisal*, 1981.

Juan José Mira, *Biografia de la Novela Policiaca*, Barcelona, 1956.

Alma Murch, *The Development of the Detective Novel*, London, 1968.

W.H. Nagel, *Lezend over Misdaad*, Leiden, 1953.

Thomas Narcejac, *Une Machine à Lire — le Roman Policier*, Paris, 1975.

Peter C. Newman, *Bronfman Dynasty*, Toronto, 1978.

William F. Nolan, *Dashiel Hammett: A Casebook*, Santa Barbara, 1969.

J. Nuttall, *Bomb Culture*, London, 1968.

Sean O'Callaghan, *The Triads*, London, 1978.

Jerry Palmer, *Thrillers*, London, 1978.

Janet Pate, *The Book of Sleuths*, London, 1977.

Otto Penzler (ed.), *The Great Detectives*, Boston, 1975.

Marc Perremond, *Marx, la Mort et les Autres*, hectogr., 1982.

R. Philmore, 'Inquest on Detective Stories', in Howard Haycraft, *op. cit.*

Dennis Porter, *The Pursuit of Crime*, New Haven, 1981.

Mario Puzo, *The Godfather Papers*, London, 1972.

Ellery Queen, *Japanese Golden Dozen*, Tokyo, 1972.

C.L. Ragghianti, *Estetica Industriali*, Milan, 1954.

Bogomil Raimov, *La Novela Negra*, Havana, 1978.

Luis Regelio Nogueras, *Por la Novela Policiaca*, Havana, 1981.

Heinz Reif (ed.), *Räuber, Volk und Obrigkeit*, Frankfurt, 1984.

Wilhelm Roth, 'Der Bürger als Verbrecher. Materialien zum deutschen Kriminalroman', in Erhard Schütz, *Zur Aktualitat des Kriminalromans*, Munich, 1978

William Ruehlmann, *Saint with a Gun: The Unlawful American Private Eye*, New York, 1974.

Charles Rycroft, 'A Detective Story: Psychoanalytical Observations', in *Psychoanalytical Quarterly*, XXVI, 1957.

Hans Sanders, *Institution Literature und Roman*, Frankfurt, 1981.

Dorothy Sayers, *Great Short Stories of Detection, Mystery and Horror*, London, 1928.

Dorothy Sayers, *Aristoteles on Detective Fiction*, London, 1936.

Dorothy Sayers, 'The Omnibus of Crime', in Howard Haycraft, *op. cit.*

Erhard Schütz Hrsg., *Zur Aktualität des Kriminalromans*, Munich, 1978.

Sutherland Scott, *Blood in their Ink: The March of the Modern Mystery Novel*, New York, 1953.

Georges Simenon, *Mémories Intimes*, Paris, 1981.

Jim Sheranko, 'The Bloody Pulps', in *The Sheranko History of Comics*, Reading, 1970.

Victor Shklovsky, 'Die Kriminalerzählung bei Conan Doyle', in Jochen Vogt, *Der Kriminalroman*, Munich, 1971.

Harrison R. Steeves, A Sober Word on the Detective Story, in Howard Haycraft, *op. cit.*

John Sutherland, *Bestsellers, Popular Fiction of the 1970s*, London, 1981.

John Sutherland, *Fiction and the Fiction Industry*, London 1980.

Julian Symons, *Bloody Murder*, (rev.ed.), Harmondsworth, 1974.

Julian Symons, *Portrait of an Artist: Conan Doyle*, London, 1979.

Alberto Tedeschi and Gian Orsi, *Piccola Enciclopedia del Giallo*, Milan, 1979.

H. Douglas Thomson, *Masters of Mystery*, London, 1931.

S.S. Van Dine, 'Twenty Rules of the Detective Story', *The American Magazine*, September, 1928.

Philip Van Doren Stern, '*The Case of the Corpse in the Blind Alley*', in Howard Haycraft, *op. cit.*

Salvador Vazquez de Parga, Los Mitos de la Novela Criminal, Barcelona, 1981.

Jochen Vogt (ed.), *Der Kriminalroman*, Munich, 1971.

Michel Vovelle, *La Mort et l'Occident de 1300 à nos jours*, Paris, 1983.

Colin Watson, *Snobbery with Violence*, London, 1979.

Nathan Weinstock, 'Een figuur die verdwijnt: de sociale bandiet', in *Tijdschrift voor Sociale Wetenschappen*, 1969, No. 1.

Raymond Williams, *The Long Revolution*, London, 1961.

Edmund Wilson, 'Who Cares Who Killed Roger Ackroyd?', in Howard Haycraft, *op. cit.*

F. *Wölcken, Der literarische Mord*, Nürenberg, 1953.

Dilys Winn, *Murder Ink*, Westbridge Books, 1978.

Th. Würtenberger, *Die deutsche Kriminalerzählung*, 1941.

Theodor Zeldin, 'Histoire des passions françaises', *Recherches*, Vol. 5, Paris, 1979.

Howard Zehr, *Crime and the Development of Modern Society*, London, 1976.

Index